W9-AQK-576

Better Homes and Gardens®

# ENCYCLOPEDIA of COOKING

*Volume 17*

Surprise those hearty, man-sized appetites in your family with unforgettable Stroganoff Steak Sandwich. Zesty, beer-marinated flank steak is complemented with onions and sour cream.

**On the cover:** Elegant is the word for this light Turkey Soufflé. A creamy, subtly seasoned dill-mushroom sauce complements the soufflé's delicate turkey flavor.

BETTER HOMES AND GARDENS BOOKS
NEW YORK • DES MOINES


Printed in the United States of America.
Special Edition. First Printing.
Library of Congress Catalog Card Number: 73-83173
SBN: 696-02037-8

**SHORTENING—1.** The preparation process of making a food short. **2.** A solid or liquid fat or oil including lard, butter, margarine, hydrogenated shortening, and vegetable oils. The main purpose of shortening is to contribute shortness to the product. For example, shortening provides tenderness to cakes, cookies, and breads; aids in leavening; and adds strength to batters. Some shortenings, such as butter or margarine, contribute flavor to the final product.

When a recipe specifies shortening, it usually means one of the solid hydrogenated vegetable shortenings. (See *Fat, Oil, Short* for additional information.)

## Cheese Loaves

*Flavored with sharp American cheese—*

**5½ to 5¾ cups sifted all-purpose flour**
**2 packages active dry yeast**
**8 ounces sharp process American cheese, shredded (2 cups)**
**2 cups milk**
**2 tablespoons sugar**
**2 tablespoons shortening**
**2 teaspoons salt**

In large mixer bowl combine *2 cups* of the flour and the yeast. In saucepan heat cheese, milk, sugar, shortening, and salt just till warm (115-120°), stirring constantly to melt cheese. Add to dry mixture in mixer bowl. Beat at low speed with electric mixer for ½ minute, scraping bowl. Beat 3 minutes at high speed. By hand, stir in enough remaining flour to make a soft dough. Turn out onto lightly floured surface and knead till smooth and elastic (5 to 8 minutes). Shape into a ball.

Place dough in lightly greased bowl, turning once to grease surface. Cover and let rise in warm place till double (45 to 60 minutes). Punch dough down; turn out on lightly floured surface. Divide dough in half. Cover and let rest 10 minutes. Shape into 2 loaves and place in two greased 8½x4½x2½-inch *or* two greased 9x5x3-inch loaf pans. Cover loaves and let rise in warm place till double (30 to 45 minutes). Bake bread at 375° till done, 30 to 35 minutes. Remove bread from pans and cool on wire racks. Makes 2 loaves cheese bread.

## Peanut Butter Bars

**½ cup shortening**
**⅔ cup chunk-style peanut butter**
**1 teaspoon vanilla**
**2 eggs**
**1½ cups brown sugar**
**1½ cups sifted all-purpose flour**
**1½ teaspoons baking powder**
**½ teaspoon salt**
**¼ cup milk**

• • •

**2 tablespoons butter or margarine, softened**
**⅓ cup chunk-style peanut butter**
**2 cups sifted confectioners' sugar**
**Light cream**

Cream shortening, ⅔ cup peanut butter, and vanilla; beat in eggs. Mix in brown sugar. Stir together flour, baking powder, and salt. Stir into creamed mixture alternately with milk. Spread mixture in a greased 13x9x2-inch baking pan. Bake at 350° till done, about 30 minutes. (Center will be slightly soft.) Cool. For frosting, cream butter or margarine and ⅓ cup peanut butter. Slowly beat in confectioners' sugar and enough light cream to make of spreading consistency. Spread frosting over cookies. Cut in bars. Makes 18 to 24 bars.

**SHORT RIB**—A less tender cut of beef from the ends of the ribs immediately below the rib section. It contains a cross section of the rib bone and has alternating layers of lean and fat. Since it is a less tender cut of beef, it should be cooked in liquid or braised. Short ribs are perfect for soups and stews. (See also *Beef*.)

## Barbecued Short Ribs

Trim excess fat from 4 pounds beef short ribs. Season. Place ribs in Dutch oven; add water to cover. Simmer, covered, till tender, about 2 hours. Drain. Place ribs on broiler pan rack.

Combine ⅓ cup catsup, 2 tablespoons molasses, 1 tablespoon lemon juice, 2 teaspoons dry mustard, ¼ teaspoon chili powder, and dash garlic powder; brush over ribs. Broil 4 to 5 inches from heat 15 minutes, turning often and brushing with the sauce. Serves 4.

## Short Rib-Vegetable Stew

**2 pounds beef short ribs**
**1/4 cup all-purpose flour**
**2 teaspoons salt**
**1/4 teaspoon pepper**
**2 tablespoons shortening**
**2 16-ounce cans tomatoes**
**2 cloves garlic, minced**
**1 tablespoon Worcestershire sauce**
**4 to 5 carrots, peeled and sliced**
**2 medium onions, sliced**
**1 medium potato, peeled and diced**
**1 1/2 teaspoons salt**
**Dash pepper**
**Parsley Dumplings**

Cut short ribs in serving-sized pieces. Combine flour, 2 teaspoons salt, and 1/4 teaspoon pepper; coat ribs with flour mixture. In Dutch oven brown meat in hot shortening. Combine tomatoes, garlic, and Worcestershire sauce; pour over ribs. Cover and simmer 1 1/2 hours.

Add carrots, onions, and potato to meat. Simmer till meat and vegetables are tender, about 45 minutes. Skim off fat. Season with salt and pepper. Thicken slightly, if desired.

For *Parsley Dumplings:* Sift together 1 cup sifted all-purpose flour, 2 teaspoons baking powder, and 1/2 teaspoon salt. Blend in 1/4 cup snipped parsley. Combine 1/2 cup milk and 2 tablespoons salad oil; add to dry ingredients, stirring just till moistened. Drop mixture from tablespoon atop bubbling stew. Cover tightly; bring to boiling. Reduce heat (don't lift cover) and simmer 15 minutes. Makes 4 or 5 servings.

## Braised Short Ribs

Trim excess fat from 3 pounds beef short ribs. Roll ribs in all-purpose flour. Brown ribs in 2 tablespoons hot shortening; spoon off fat. Season with 1 teaspoon salt and dash pepper. Add 1 medium onion, sliced, and 1/2 cup water. Cover; simmer till tender, 2 to 2 1/2 hours. (Add more water, if needed.) Remove meat; keep hot.

Prepare *Onion Gravy:* Skim fat from meat juices, reserving 2 tablespoons fat. Measure juices, and add enough water to make 2 cups. Brown 1/4 cup sugar in reserved fat. Add 2 medium onions, thinly sliced; cook till tender.

Shred a cabbage for coleslaw by first cutting the head of cabbage in half. Then, use a sharp knife to cut the cabbage in fine shreds.

Push the onions to one side. Add 2 tablespoons all-purpose flour; brown the flour slightly. Stir in meat juices, 1 tablespoon vinegar, and 1/4 teaspoon Kitchen Bouquet. Return to heat; cook and stir till gravy thickens and bubbles. Boil 2 to 3 minutes. Season to taste with salt and pepper. Serve gravy with short ribs. Makes 6 servings.

**SHOYU** ***(shō' yōō)***—The Japanese word for soy sauce. (See also *Soy Sauce.*)

**SHRED**—To cut foods with a knife or grater or to tear foods into thin strips or slivers. For example, cabbage, lettuce, and carrots are often shredded for salads. Cheese is another food that is shredded and used as an ingredient in recipes.

**SHREDDED WHEAT**—A whole wheat cereal made of long, thin shreds of cooked wheat that are shaped into large, oblong, or round biscuits or into bite-sized squares. One shredded wheat biscuit adds 85 calories to the diet in addition to some protein, phosphorus, and B vitamins. When used as an ingredient, shredded wheat adds both flavor and crisp texture. (See also *Cereal.*)

**SHRIMP**—A small, long-tailed shellfish related to the crab and lobster. The shrimp resembles a lobster in miniature. It has 10 legs, tiny claws, an arched back, and a segmented shell. The shell is grayish green, pink, red, or brownish red. The meat is white and has a tender texture and a sweet taste that are popular with Americans.

Shrimp has been included in many countries' cuisines. The Greeks, Romans, and Chinese began using it centuries ago. Today, shrimp is still a prominent food in typical Italian and oriental dishes.

In the United States, shrimp were first available to the people who lived near the Gulf and Pacific coasts. Only within the last century have Americans throughout the nation had access to supplies of shrimp. Developments in canning, freezing, and shipping have made this possible.

**How shrimp live:** Shrimp live along muddy inshore and offshore waters. In the United States, they inhabit the waters along the Gulf coast from North Carolina to Texas and along the Pacific coast from San Francisco Bay to Alaska. Shrimp also are found in the waters off the coasts of South America, Japan, Europe, and Asia.

The shrimp of each area possess distinguishing characteristics. Those from the Gulf of Mexico are large, and are white, brown, red, or pink. Pacific shrimp are much smaller and are usually pink. South American shrimp look brownish red.

All shrimp, regardless of the area in which they are found, lead similar lives. The life cycle begins during the spawning season, which takes place in offshore waters from March to September. The tiny shrimp eggs settle to the bottom of the ocean rather than being carried by the mother as are some shellfish eggs. Within a few weeks time, the eggs hatch and the larvae return to the water's surface. The young shrimp, like other shellfish, undergo

*Grill shrimp on a hibachi*

Baste Sweet-Sour Sauced Shrimp with pimiento-dotted sauce. Use small shrimp for appetizers and large ones for an entrée.

a series of changes, and eventually they develop into a form that looks similar to that of the adult shrimp.

The developing shrimp move toward the coastline and go to the bottom of inland waters and rivers. These shrimp are caught in harvest from August to December.

As winter approaches, the smaller shrimp stay near the coast, but the larger ones travel offshore toward warmer waters. These large shrimp are the ones taken in offshore waters from March to June.

Shrimp are caught by the crews of shrimp boats or trawlers, who drag nets along the bottom of the water. The majority of the catch goes to processing plants where the head and thorax are removed (these parts have very little meat). Then, machinery separates the shrimp by size, removes the shells, and cleans the shrimp. Machinery also applies breading to some of the shrimp. Then, they are canned or frozen for nationwide distribution.

***Nutritional value:*** Shrimp, like other fish and shellfish, are a good source of protein. The B vitamins and minerals (calcium, phosphorus, copper, and iodine) are also present. The calories in a serving of shrimp depend on the method of cooking used and the sauce or breading added. A 3½-ounce serving, uncooked, has 90 calories, while french-frying increases the calorie count to 225. If frozen shrimp are purchased breaded, a 3½-ounce serving, uncooked, will average about 140 calories.

**Buying shrimp:** Shrimp on the market range from fresh, whole ones to frozen, breaded tails. Whole shrimp are rarely found except along the coast. Most of the fresh ones are sold headless, peeled or unpeeled, and with sand vein still present or deveined. The name "green shrimp," which is applied to some shrimp, does not refer to color; rather, it means that they have not been cooked. When buying fresh shrimp, look for those with a mild odor and firm, glossy shells that fit the body.

Canned shrimp—cooked, peeled, and deveined—come in both dry pack and wet pack. Smoked or dried shrimp, shrimp paste, shrimp in cocktail sauce, and frozen entrées are also available.

Frozen shrimp come in various combinations of processing—cooked or raw, peeled or unpeeled, deveined or with vein, and breaded or plain. They may be frozen together or individually. The separate ones are convenient especially for those who cook only a portion of the package at a time. The number of shrimp needed can be removed without having to thaw the whole package; the remainder can then be returned to the freezer for future use.

Frozen entrées, such as shrimp creole and chow mein, and frozen soups are among the many products that can be found in the super market.

When purchasing shrimp, allow approximately 6 of them per person or ¼ pound of shrimp without shells per person.

***How Much Shrimp You Need***

| Shrimp in 1 pound | |
|---|---|
| Size | Number of raw shrimp in shell from 1 pound |
| Jumbo size | 15 to 18 |
| Average size | 26 to 30 |
| Tiny | 60 or more |

| Buy in shell or shelled | |
|---|---|
| Amount needed | Amount to buy |
| For each 1 cup cleaned, cooked shrimp | 12 ounces raw shrimp in shell *or*<br>7 or 8 ounces frozen shelled shrimp *or*<br>1 4½- or 5-ounce can shrimp |

| Shrimp in casserole or sauce | |
|---|---|
| Servings | Amount needed |
| For 4 servings of casserole or creamy sauce (approximate) | 1 pound shrimp in shell *or*<br>1⅓ cups cleaned, cooked shrimp *or*<br>1 or 2 4½- or 5-ounce cans (1 or 2 cups) shrimp |

**Storing shrimp:** Fresh shrimp should be wrapped and stored in the coldest section of the refrigerator for a day or two. For longer storage, freeze uncooked, headless shrimp either with or without shells.

Be sure commercially frozen and home-frozen shrimp are wrapped in moisture-vaporproof material and sealed securely.

Use frozen shrimp within three months. If possible, cook them while still frozen. If you can't do this, thaw shrimp in the refrigerator and use them immediately. Never refreeze shrimp.

**Cleaning shrimp:** Shrimp are cleaned either before or after boiling. Those cleaned before boiling have a more delicate flavor, while those cleaned after boiling have a more attractive appearance. The choice depends on personal taste.

When cleaning fresh shrimp, remove the head and thorax if the shrimp are whole. Peel off the shell and devein the shrimp. Butterfly large shrimp for frying by cutting to but not through the back.

Devein shrimp by making a slit along the arch of the back with a knife. Rinse under cold water and remove the black vein.

***The secret of cooking shrimp***

Cook shrimp only a short time. They're done when firm and a reddish pink color. Avoid overcooking because this shrinks them, and avoid rinsing with cold water as this toughens them. Cool and then refrigerate.

**Cooking shrimp:** Shrimp are delicious cooked in a number of ways. The most popular methods are frying and boiling. However, other methods should be explored, for there are many delicious ways of preparing shrimp. Shrimp can be baked, broiled, barbecued, or made into casseroles, salads, appetizers, stuffings, pizzas, and breakfast entrées. (See also *Shellfish*.)

## Fresh Cooked Shrimp

In large saucepan combine 6 cups water, 2 tablespoons salt, 2 tablespoons vinegar, 2 bay leaves, 1 teaspoon mixed pickling spices, and 2 branches celery; bring to boiling.

Add 2 pounds fresh or frozen shrimp in shells or shelled. Heat the mixture to boiling, then lower heat and simmer gently till the shrimp turn pink, about 1 to 3 minutes. Drain. If cooked in shell, peel shrimp and remove black vein that runs down the back.

*Note:* When cooking shrimp for highly seasoned dishes, omit the vinegar and the spices.

## Jiffy Shrimp Skillet

In skillet place one 10-ounce can frozen condensed cream of shrimp soup, thawed; add ¾ cup water and stir to blend. Cover; bring just to boiling. Stir in ⅔ cup uncooked packaged precooked rice; 7 or 8 ounces frozen, shelled shrimp, ⅓ cup chopped celery, ⅓ cup chopped green pepper, ¼ teaspoon salt, and ½ to 1 teaspoon curry powder. Cover; return to boiling. Reduce heat; simmer till rice and shrimp are done, 10 minutes, stirring occasionally.

• Just before serving the shrimp mixture, add ⅓ cup sliced, pitted ripe olives. Sprinkle with 2 tablespoons toasted, slivered almonds. Makes 3 or 4 servings.

Arrange individual servings of French Shrimp in Shells around a dish of green vegetables, and present the meal at the table. This simple menu makes an unbeatably delicious combination.

## French Shrimp in Shells

**1 pound small, shelled shrimp**
**1/4 cup butter or margarine**
**3 tablespoons all-purpose flour**
**1 1/2 cups milk**
**1/2 teaspoon salt**
**Dash pepper**
**Dash paprika**
**1/4 cup dry sherry**
**Grated Parmesan cheese**

Cook shrimp; drain. Melt butter in saucepan; stir in flour. Add milk; cook and stir till thickened. Stir in salt, pepper, paprika, sherry, and shrimp. Pour into 5 baking shells; sprinkle each with 1 tablespoon Parmesan cheese. Place under broiler 3 to 4 inches from heat; broil till cheese browns. Makes 5 servings.

## Shrimp de Jonghe

**2 pounds shelled shrimp**
**1/2 cup butter or margarine**
**2 cloves garlic, minced**
**1/3 cup snipped parsley**
**1/2 teaspoon paprika**
**Dash cayenne pepper**
**1/2 cup dry white wine**

• • •

**2 cups soft bread crumbs**

Cook shrimp; arrange in an 11 3/4x7 1/2x1 3/4-inch baking dish. Melt butter; add garlic, parsley, paprika, cayenne, and wine; mix. Stir in bread crumbs. Spread crumb mixture over shrimp.

Bake at 350° till crumbs brown, about 25 minutes. Sprinkle with more snipped parsley, if desired. Makes 6 to 8 servings.

## Shrimp à l'Imperatrice

**1 cup mayonnaise**
**1 teaspoon dry mustard**
**3 tablespoons chopped, canned pimiento**
**1/4 cup finely diced green pepper**
**1/2 teaspoon salt**
**1 1/2 pounds shrimp in shells, cooked and shelled, *or* 2 4 1/2-ounce cans shrimp**
**3 avocados, peeled and halved**
**2 teaspoons fine dry bread crumbs**
**Paprika**
**Lemon wedges**

Thoroughly combine mayonnaise and mustard. Add chopped pimiento, green pepper, and salt; mix well. Fold in shrimp. Fill each avocado half, cut side up, with shrimp mixture (you may have to slice off bottom of avocados to get them to stand upright). Sprinkle tops with bread crumbs and paprika. Serve hot or cold. To serve hot, bake at 350° till heated through, about 10 to 15 minutes. To serve cold, chill shrimp mixture before filling avocado halves. Pass lemon wedges. Makes 6 servings.

## Sweet-Sour Sauced Shrimp

*Grill these outdoors for a rare treat—*

**1 cup sugar**
**1/2 cup white vinegar**
**1 tablespoon chopped green pepper**
**1 tablespoon chopped, canned pimiento**
**1/2 teaspoon salt**
**2 teaspoons cornstarch**
**1 tablespoon cold water**
**1 teaspoon paprika**
**Shelled, raw shrimp**

In saucepan mix sugar, vinegar, 1/2 cup water, green pepper, pimiento, and salt. Simmer 5 minutes. Combine cornstarch and cold water; add to hot mixture. Cook and stir till sauce is thickened and bubbly. Cool. Add paprika.

Cook the shelled, raw shrimp on fine wire grill over *hot* coals till done, about 6 to 8 minutes, turning once and brushing often with sweet-sour sauce. *Don't overcook!* Pass extra sauce with the shrimp. Makes 1 1/2 cups sauce.

## Shrimp à la King

*Make ahead and freeze till ready to serve—*

**1 7-ounce package frozen, shelled shrimp**
**1 3-ounce can sliced mushrooms, drained**
**1/4 cup chopped green pepper**
**1/4 cup butter or margarine**

• • •

**2 tablespoons all-purpose flour**
**1/2 teaspoon salt**
**Several dashes white pepper**
**2 cups milk**
**1 tablespoon lemon juice**
**6 to 8 toast cups**

Cook shrimp according to package directions; drain. In medium saucepan cook mushrooms and green pepper in butter or margarine till tender. Blend in flour, salt, and white pepper. Add milk all at once. Cook and stir till thickened and bubbly. Stir in shrimp and lemon juice. Heat through; serve in toast cups.

*Or* pour mixture into 1-quart casserole; cool. Cover and freeze. When ready to serve, bake frozen casserole, covered, at 375° till heated through, about 50 to 60 minutes. Stir occasionally while heating. Makes 6 to 8 servings.

## Shrimp and Rice Deluxe

**1/2 cup milk**
**1 cup water**
**1 10 1/2-ounce can condensed cream of celery soup**
**1 7-ounce package frozen rice and peas with mushrooms**
**1 4 1/2- or 5-ounce can shrimp, drained, *or* 1 1/2 cups cooked shrimp**
**2 tablespoons snipped parsley**
**1/2 teaspoon curry powder**
**Toasted slivered almonds**

In a 2-quart saucepan gradually blend the milk and water into cream of celery soup. Add frozen rice and peas with mushrooms, shrimp, the 2 tablespoons snipped parsley, and curry powder. Cover and simmer gently for 30 minutes. Stir mixture occasionally. Garnish with toasted, slivered almonds. Makes 4 to 6 servings.

## Shrimp Sandwiches

*Cut into tiny triangles for tea sandwiches or into halves for a luncheon entrée—*

**1 3-ounce package cream cheese, softened**
**2 tablespoons mayonnaise or salad dressing**

. . .

**1 tablespoon catsup**
**1 teaspoon prepared mustard**
**Dash garlic powder**

. . .

**1 cup chopped, cooked shrimp**
**1/4 cup finely chopped celery**
**1 teaspoon finely chopped onion**
**8 to 10 slices lightly buttered white bread**

Blend cream cheese with mayonnaise or salad dressing; mix in catsup, prepared mustard, and garlic powder. Stir in shrimp, celery, and onion. Spread mixture between bread slices. For tea sandwiches, use 10 slices; for luncheon size, size, use 8 slices. Trim crusts from bread, if desired. Cut each tea sandwich diagonally in 4 triangles; cut luncheon size in half. Makes 4 luncheon or 20 tea sandwiches.

Spear a Gourmet Shrimp on wooden picks for dipping into a special sauce. A chafing dish keeps the appetizers warm.

## Shrimp-Curry Luncheon

**1 avocado, peeled and sliced**
**1 tablespoon lime juice**
**1 1/2 teaspoons butter or margarine**
**1/2 teaspoon curry powder**
**1 small tomato, peeled and chopped**
**2 tablespoons chopped onion**
**3/4 cup cooked shrimp**
**1/2 cup dairy sour cream**
**2 English muffins, split**

Brush avocado slices with lime juice; heat at 300° for 5 to 10 minutes.

Melt butter in small saucepan; add curry, 1/2 teaspoon salt, tomato, and onion. Cook till onion is tender, 5 minutes. Add shrimp; heat through. Stir in sour cream; heat, *but do not boil.* Toast muffins. Top muffins with warm avocado; spoon shrimp curry over. Serves 2.

## Shrimp-Cheese Fondue

**1 10-ounce can frozen condensed cream of shrimp soup, thawed**
**1/2 cup milk**
**2 teaspoons instant minced onion**
**1/4 teaspoon dry mustard**
**1 pound process Swiss cheese, shredded (4 cups)**
**2 tablespoons dry sherry**
**French bread or hard rolls**

In a saucepan heat soup and milk till blended. Stir in onion, mustard, and Swiss cheese. Heat and stir till cheese melts. Stir in wine, Serve immediately in fondue pot or chafing dish. Cut bread in bite-sized pieces with crust on each. Spear cube on long-handled fork and swirl in cheese mixture. Serves 6 to 8.

## Gourmet Shrimp

Combine 1 cup catsup, 1/4 cup sauterne, and 2 tablespoons snipped parsley; chill thoroughly.

Melt 1/4 cup butter or margarine in skillet or blazer pan of chafing dish. Add 1 clove garlic, minced, and 1 teaspoon dried dillweed. Cook several minutes. Add 2 cups shelled, raw shrimp and cook till shrimp turn pink, about 5 to 10 minutes. Turn occasionally. Salt to taste. Serve with chilled sauce. Serves 4.

## Shrimp Sauce

*Try this sauce with egg dishes—*

Melt 2 tablespoons butter; blend in 2 tablespoons all-purpose flour. Stir in one 10-ounce can frozen condensed cream of shrimp soup, thawed, and 1 soup can milk. Cook and stir till bubbly. Add ½ cup shredded sharp process American cheese; stir to melt. Makes 3 cups.

**SHRIMP SPICE**—A blend of seasonings, also called shrimp boil or crab boil. Commercial blends of shrimp spice contain a combination of red pepper, bay leaf, mustard seed, allspice, clove, black pepper, savory, and dillseed, all in whole form. Placing shrimp spice in the boiling water with shrimp, crab, or other seafood gives the food extra flavor. Bundling the spices together in a cheesecloth bag makes them easy to remove at the end of cooking time.

**SHRUB**—A beverage made of fruit juice, sugar, and sometimes alcohol. The juice, usually orange or lemon, gives the drink a tart flavor, and the sugar adds sweetness. Rum or brandy can be added for an alcoholic drink. These mixtures are drunk cool from tumblers either straight or diluted.

Shrubs have been a popular drink since colonial times. The pioneers were fond of the refreshing flavor, and they were able to store the drink year-round.

**SHUCK**—**1.** The outer covering on corn, nuts, oysters, and clams. **2.** To remove this covering. To shuck corn, peel the husks off the ears. Shuck nuts by cracking and removing the shell. Shuck oysters and clams by cutting around the shell, forcing it open, and cutting out the muscle.

**SIDECAR**—An alcoholic cocktail made of brandy, lemon juice, and orange liqueur. (See also *Wines and Spirits*.)

**SIEVE** ***(siv)***—**1.** A circular utensil with a wire mesh or fine holes. **2.** To force food through a sieve or a sifter.

Sieves come in various sizes. Most of them have a handle attached. The bottom and sides are of wire mesh.

Sieve foods by pushing them through the wire mesh. Begin with utensil about half full and press with back of a large spoon.

Sieving serves various purposes in the home. Drain liquids from a food by balancing the sieve over a container and pouring the food into the sieve. Purée foods by forcing them through the sieve. Recipes for cheesecake, for example, often call for cottage cheese to be puréed. This may be done with a sieve.

A sieve can even double as a sifter. Shake flour or dry ingredients through the mesh part of the sieve. Use a spoon to press the food through, if necessary.

**SIFT**—To force foods through a sieve or sifter. Many functions in the kitchen involve sifting. Dry ingredients are blended together, foods are fluffed, and foreign particles are removed. Lumps are broken up, and foods are sprinkled, such as confectioners' sugar over a cake.

Follow correct procedures when sifting flour—sift the flour onto waxed paper or a plate; spoon lightly into a measuring cup designed for dry ingredients, being careful not to pack or shake the cup; and level off with a knife or spatula. This will give a measurement that is consistent with that used in testing the recipe. Thus, the best results will be achieved.

**SIFTER**—A small kitchen utensil that is similar to a sieve or a strainer, used for aerating flour or confectioners' sugar. Sifters, in the form of variously sized metal cups, have a screen bottom through which the flour or sugar is forced. Revolving disks or wires rub across the fine mesh screen bottom propelled by a lever which is most often connected to the handle of the sifter.

Many baked products are dependent upon the use of a sifter for producing a light and airy product. For example, a sifter is very important in the making of a light and tender angel food or sponge cake. The dry ingredients are usually sifted together three times so as much air as possible is incorporated into the mixture.

Besides aerating dry ingredients, a sifter breaks up or holds back possible lumps, as in the case of confectioners' sugar, which is often used in making a smooth, creamy frosting. Also, a sifter is used to blend together dry ingredients, such as flour, leavening agents, salt, and spices before they are combined with the liquid ingredients. (See also *Equipment.*)

**SIMMER**—To cook food in liquid at a temperature of 185 to 210 degrees, where bubbles form at a slow rate and burst before reaching the surface. Simmering is a slow method of cooking and is preferred over faster cooking temperatures for a number of reasons: High protein foods, such as fish, meat, and eggs toughen at higher temperatures, which makes simmering a more suitable cookery method. Soups and sauces develop a rich flavor and smooth consistency if allowed to simmer on the range for several hours. And tougher cuts of meat become surprisingly tender and dried fruits turn out plump and juicy when allowed to simmer. Foods also retain their shapes better during gentle simmering.

**SIMNEL CAKE** ***(sim' nuhl)***—A rich, fruitcake with a filling and topping of almond paste. A British Lenten cake, it is also called Mothering Sunday Cake because, years ago, indentured servant girls were allowed to bake the simnel cake to take to their mothers on the fourth Sunday in Lent —their only visiting day. The cake is now popular at holiday times as a fruitcake.

## Simnel Cake

**½ cup butter**
**⅓ cup sugar**
**3 eggs**

• • •

**½ cup raisins**
**½ cup currants**
**¼ cup mixed candied fruits and peels**
**2 teaspoons grated lemon peel**
**1 cup sifted all-purpose flour**
**½ teaspoon baking powder**
**½ teaspoon salt**
**½ teaspoon ground nutmeg**
**¼ teaspoon ground cinnamon**
**1 tablespoon water**
**1 tablespoon light molasses**

• • •

**8 ounces almond paste**
**1 beaten egg**
**Confectioners' Icing**

In small mixer bowl cream together butter and sugar. Add eggs, one at a time, beating well after each addition. Combine raisins, currants, mixed fruits and peels, and lemon peel; set aside. Sift together flour, baking powder, salt, nutmeg, and cinnamon; sprinkle over fruits, tossing to coat. Stir into creamed mixture. Add water and molasses; mix well.

Pour *half* of the batter into greased and floured 8x1½-inch layer cake pan. Divide almond paste into thirds. Roll ⅓ of the paste between waxed paper to a 7-inch round; remove waxed paper. Place almond paste round on cake batter in pan. Cover with remaining batter. Bake at 325° till done, 40 to 45 minutes. Cool.

Roll another ⅓ of the almond paste to a 7-inch round; place atop cake. Shape remaining almond paste into 11 balls; arrange around top edge of cake. Brush with beaten egg; bake at 400° till golden, 7 to 8 minutes. When cool, drizzle with *Confectioners' Icing*: Combine 1 cup sifted confectioners' sugar, ½ teaspoon vanilla, and 1 to 2 tablespoons milk.

**SIMPLE SYRUP**—Equal parts or two parts granulated sugar to one part water cooked for five minutes to make a thin syrup. It is used in some canning, as sweetener for punches and drinks, and as a glaze for some breads and coffee breads.

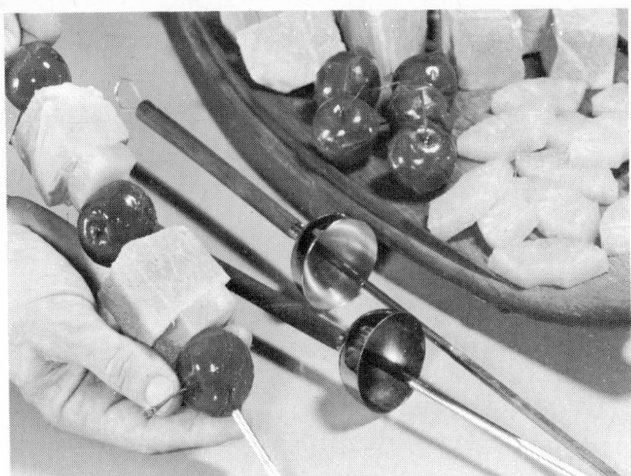

Thread chunks of fruit and meat onto skewwer for broiling. Make sure the food pieces are centered so they will cook evenly.

**SIPPET** *(sip' it)*—Small triangles of freshly made toast that are used to complete or garnish a food, such as seafood Newburg or creamed chicken dishes.

**SIRLOIN**—A cut of meat—steak or roast—from the hip area of the hindquarters of beef, pork, lamb, or veal. Often a hip bone is present—round, flat, or wedge in shape. However, some steaks and most roasts are boneless. The sirloin is usually an excellent cut of meat.

Sirloin steaks are broiled, and high quality roasts are roasted. Less-tender roasts are cooked with moist heat. (See *Beef, Meat, Steak* for additional information.)

## Braised Sirloin Roast

Sprinkle one 3- to 4-pound beef sirloin tip roast lightly with 2 tablespoons all-purpose flour and rub in. In Dutch oven, brown roast slowly on all sides in 2 tablespoons shortening. Season with 2 teaspoons salt and 1/4 teaspoon pepper. Add 1 medium onion, sliced; 2 bay leaves; 1 clove garlic, minced; and 1/2 cup hot water to roast. Cover and cook at 350° till meat is almost tender, about 2 hours.

Add 8 small onions, peeled; 8 medium carrots, peeled; and 8 small potatoes, peeled. Sprinkle vegetables with 1 1/2 teaspoons salt. Cook, covered, till meat and vegetables are tender, 1 1/2 hours. Make gravy. Serves 6 to 8.

## Sirloin Tip Roast

**1 3- to 4-pound sirloin tip roast**
**2 tablespoons all-purpose flour**
**2 tablespoons shortening**
**2 teaspoons salt**
**1/2 cup pineapple juice**
**1 tablespoon instant minced onion**
**1 tablespoon lemon juice**
**1 teaspoon Italian salad dressing mix**
**1 teaspoon Worcestershire sauce**
**1/8 teaspoon pepper**
**Gravy**

Sprinkle meat lightly with flour; brown slowly on all sides in hot shortening in roasting pan. Season with salt. Combine pineapple juice and next 5 ingredients; pour over meat. Cover; roast at 325° till meat is tender, about 2 to 2 3/4 hours. Remove to serving platter. Allow 3 or 4 servings per pound of meat.

To prepare *Gravy*, pour pan juices into large measuring cup. Skim off excess fat; return 1 1/2 cups juices to pan. Combine 1/2 cup cold water and 1/4 cup all-purpose flour in shaker; shake well. Stir into juices; cook, stirring constantly, till gravy is thickened and bubbly. If desired, add a little Kitchen Bouquet for a richer, brown color. Makes 2 cups gravy.

**SKATE**—A saltwater fish that has large side winglike fins. These Pacific coast fish have a broad, flat body and measure two to eight feet in length.

The fins are delicious when poached or fried. To eat these fins, scrape off the flesh with the knife and fork instead of cutting it into bites. (See also *Fish.*)

**SKEWER**—**1.** Short, sharp metal or wooden pins used to hold stuffed meat roasts, chops, or fish together as they cook. **2.** Long metal or bamboo pins used for threading food to form kabobs for broiling.

When used to hold together the stuffing in poultry, the small metal skewers are laced together with heavy cord. When used in fish or chops, the metal skewers act as pins to hold in the stuffing. Wooden skewers are used by butchers to hold together boned meats or roasts with pockets cut in them for stuffing.

Skewers used for kabobs, called *brochettes* in French, vary in length. Foods, such as meat chunks and vegetable or fruit pieces, are threaded onto the long metal pins for broiling. Because it is an attractive and unusual way to serve food, marinated fruits or vegetables are sometimes strung on short skewers for serving.

## Marinated Skewered Fruit

**1 $20\frac{1}{2}$-ounce can pineapple chunks**
**$\frac{1}{4}$ cup honey**
**1 tablespoon brandy**
**1 teaspoon snipped fresh mint *or* dried mint flakes**
**1 apple, cut in wedges**
**1 pear, cut in wedges**
**1 nectarine, cut in wedges**

Drain pineapple chunks, reserving the syrup. To the syrup add honey, brandy, and snipped fresh mint *or* dried mint flakes. Place apple, pear, and nectarine wedges in shallow dish; add the honey mixture. Marinate in refrigerator 2 to 3 hours, turning fruit wedges occasionally. Thread on skewers, or serve in sherbet dishes with marinade. Makes 4 servings.

Use skewers for serving marinated fruit chunks. Select fresh or canned fruits of assorted colors for an interesting effect.

**SKILLET**—A frying pan, sometimes called a spider, an old-fashioned name that dates back to the days when iron skillets were made with three legs.

Made of metal, ceramic, or enamel, skillets have a long handle and usually are quite shallow. Electric skillets, controlled by an adjustable thermostat, maintain a constant cooking temperature.

Skillets are most popularly used for panfrying, panbroiling, and sautéeing. They are sometimes appropriate for preparing stews, one-dish meals, vegetables, and desserts. (See *Appliance, Pots and Pans* for additional information.)

**SKIM**—**1.** To remove floating particles from a liquid with the aid of a flat, perforated utensil. **2.** To remove the cream that rises to the surface of whole milk that has not been homogenized.

The floating particles, in the form of a layer, are often referred to as the foam, froth, or scum. Examples of skimming include removing the foam that forms on the top of jam or jelly during the cooking process, and removing the floating fat from the surface of soups or stews before they are spooned into serving dishes.

**SKIM MILK**—Whole milk from which almost all the fat has been removed. States have different standards as to the minimum percentage of nonfat milk solids or total milk solids that skim milk must have.

In the shopper's mind, there often is some confusion about those milks which contain less fat than whole milk. Carefully reading the labeling of each of them individually, one can see the differences in each type of milk.

*Skim milk* has the least amount of milk fat—ordinarily 0.5 percent or less milk fat content. *Low fat milk* has slightly more fat than skim milk—0.5 to 1.9 percent, while *two percent milk* has just a bit more fat—two percent, as the name indicates. Most of these milks are usually enriched with nonfat milk solids.

The nutritive value of skim milk is less than that of whole milk as is the calorie count. Because of the reduction in fats, skim milk contains lesser amounts of vitamin A, although this vitamin is frequently added along with vitamin D in commercial production. Other nutrients in skim milk are the same as in whole milk.

Among skim milk products are instant nonfat dry milk and evaporated skim milk. Skim milk is used to make some cheeses, cottage cheese, and cultured buttermilk. It is also a popular beverage and recipe ingredient for those people who find it necessary to count calories. One cup of enriched skim milk contains about 105 calories, while one cup whole milk provides 160 calories. (See also *Milk*.)

## Raspberry Bavarian Cake

*A make-ahead dessert that is low in calories—*

**1 7/8-ounce package low-calorie raspberry-flavored gelatin (2 envelopes)**
**1 cup evaporated skim milk**
**1 cup fresh raspberries, sweetened *or* 1 10-ounce package frozen raspberries, thawed and drained**
**1 10-inch angel cake**

Dissolve gelatin in 2 cups *boiling* water. Chill till partially set. Meanwhile, place evaporated skim milk in shallow pan; freeze just till ice crystals form around edges. In chilled mixer bowl, beat milk with electric beater till stiff; fold milk into partially set gelatin. Gently fold in fresh or thawed raspberries.

Cut angel cake into 3 layers. Spread about 1¼ cups of the raspberry mixture between each cake layer; spread sides and top of cake with remaining mixture. Chill till serving time.

## Banana Milk Shake

*Fresh banana flavor in a low-calorie snack—*

**1 medium-large banana**
**1 cup skim milk**
**Noncaloric sweetener equal to 1 tablespoon sugar**

Peel banana; wrap in foil and freeze. Cut frozen banana into chunks. Place milk and sweetener in blender container. Gradually add banana; blend till smooth. Makes 2 servings.

**SKIRRET** ***(skir' it)***—An Asiatic pot herb that is culivated in Europe for its sweet, edible, tuberous roots that resemble a cluster of small parsnips.

**SLAW**—The shortened name for the shredded cabbage salad tossed with mayonnaise or vinegar-type dressing. It is most often called coleslaw. (See also *Coleslaw*.)

**SLICE**—**1.** A flat piece, thin or thick as desired, cut from or across a larger piece of food, such as a roast of meat, whole carrot, loaf of bread, or cake. **2.** To cut into flat pieces, usually with a knife.

**SLING**—An alcoholic drink popular in tropical countries. Although gin is most frequently used in a sling, it often is prepared with whiskey or brandy. The drink is a combination of liquor, confectioners' sugar, fruit peel or juice, and ice. A Singapore Sling contains gin and cherry-flavored brandy. (See also *Cocktail*.)

## Singapore Sling

In highball glass combine cracked ice, ½ ounce cherry-flavored brandy, ½ ounce lemon juice, 1 teaspoon confectioners' sugar, and 1½ to 2 jiggers gin. Fill glass with cold water or carbonated water; stir. Garnish with maraschino cherry and orange slice, if desired. Serve with straws. Makes 1 serving.

Vegetables, such as yellow squash, are often sliced before cooking. A sharp knife and cutting board ensure smooth, even slices.

**SLIT**—A small, narrow incision made into a food to allow steam to escape. When preparing a two-crust pie, several slits are made in the top layer of the pastry to allow steam to escape during cooking. Slits are sometimes cut into a roast, such as leg of lamb, beef, or ham, as seasonings, such as garlic, herbs, or spices, are inserted to add flavor during roasting.

**SLIVER**—**1.** A long, thin piece of such foods as almonds, cheese, fruits, vegetables, or meats. **2.** To cut food in long, thin pieces.

Use a sharp knife or coarse grater blade to cut the slivers. Slivered almonds are among the most popular toppings for such desserts as ice cream and for many main dishes. Slivered fruits and vegetables, as well as meat and cheese, add interest to crisp, tossed salads.

## Tuna-Noodle Casserole

*Slivered almonds add a crunchy topping to creamy tuna and noodle casserole—*

**6 ounces medium noodles (3 cups)**
**1 6½- or 7-ounce can tuna, drained**
**½ cup mayonnaise or salad dressing**
**1 cup sliced celery**
**⅓ cup chopped onion**
**¼ cup chopped green pepper**
**¼ cup chopped, canned pimiento, drained**
**½ teaspoon salt**
**1 10½-ounce can condensed cream of celery soup**
**½ cup milk**
**4 ounces sharp process American cheese, shredded (1 cup)**
**½ cup slivered almonds, toasted**

Cook noodles according to package directions; drain. Combine noodles, tuna, mayonnaise, celery, onion, green pepper, pimiento, and salt.

In saucepan blend soup with milk; heat and stir till smooth. Stir in cheese; heat and stir till cheese melts. Stir into noodle mixture.

Turn mixture into 2-quart casserole. Sprinkle casserole with almonds. Bake, uncovered, at 425° for 20 minutes. Makes 6 servings.

**SLIVOVITZ** ***(sliv' uh vits, -wits, shliv'-)***—A golden brown plum brandy made in Balkan countries, particularly Yugoslavia. The brandy is doubly distilled, aged for a year, after which more plums are added. Slivovitz is the national beverage of two of the Yugoslavian republics, Bosnia and Serbia. (See also *Brandy*.)

**SLOE** ***(slō)***—A small, wild, plumlike fruit of the blackthorn, a European bush of the rose family. The bush grows in the southern and midwestern sections of the United States and is known by other names, including haw bush and bullace tree.

Although the astringent fruit is edible, sloe is rarely gathered for eating as a fresh fruit. The tart, bluish black fruit is used primarily for flavoring sloe gin, although it is also for use in making jams, jellies, and some kinds of conserves.

**SLOE GIN**—A liqueur made by steeping sloe berries in gin. The liqueur takes on the flavor and color of the berries. (See *Gin, Liqueur* for additional information.)

**SMEARCASE (SMIERCASE) CHEESE**—The Pennsylvania Dutch name for creamed cottage cheese. It means "spread cheese."

**SMELT**—A small, slender fish with silvery, olive green coloring. Smelts are usually seven or eight inches long and weigh about 1½ to 2 ounces. The rich-flavored smelts can be fat or lean, and either freshwater or saltwater fish.

Smelts have been abundant along both the Atlantic and Pacific coasts for centuries. They were caught by Indians and used for food and trading purposes. The Pacific coast Indians dried one oily type and burned it for light. And in 1906, smelts were planted in the Great Lakes to feed the salmon that were introduced into those waters. The salmon did not survive, but the smelt flourished.

Like their relative, the salmon, smelt travel up rivers and streams to spawn. This annual event occurs when the ice begins to break. At this time, when the smelts are running, people throng to the river banks to scoop up fish with all types of makeshift equipment.

For those who are not near streams to catch their own, smelt is available fresh, frozen, and canned at the market. Most of these are whole or dressed. Precooked and breaded smelt are also available in the frozen-food section.

Smelt is usually cooked whole by frying, broiling, baking, boiling, or steaming. Before cooking, four or five fish have about 100 calories if fresh, and 200 calories if canned. (See also *Fish*.)

### Smelts

**1 pound fresh or frozen smelts**
**1/4 cup milk**
**1/2 cup cornmeal**
**1/2 teaspoon salt**
**1/4 cup butter or margarine**
• • •
**2 tablespoons snipped parsley**
**Tartar sauce**
**Lemon juice**

Clean fresh smelts. (If using frozen smelts, thaw them.) Rinse smelts thoroughly and wipe dry. Dip smelts in milk, then in mixture of cornmeal and salt. In large skillet cook the smelts in butter or margarine till done, about 5 minutes on each side. Sprinkle snipped parsley over smelts and serve with tartar sauce or lemon juice. Makes 2 or 3 servings.

### Smelts in Barbecue Sauce

**1 pound fresh or frozen smelts**
**1 8-ounce can tomato sauce**
**1/2 cup chopped onion**
**2 tablespoons brown sugar**
**2 tablespoons vinegar**
**1 tablespoon Worcestershire sauce**
**1 tablespoon water**
**2 teaspoons prepared mustard**
**1/4 teaspoon salt**

Thaw frozen smelts; clean, rinse, and wipe dry. Combine all ingredients *except* smelts. Marinate smelts in tomato mixture, covered, in refrigerator for several hours. In large skillet bring smelts and tomato mixture to boiling. Reduce heat and simmer, uncovered, till fish are done, 8 to 10 minutes. Makes 3 or 4 servings.

**SMITANE**—Indicates that sour cream is one of the ingredients in a dish when used in a recipe title. It is a French variation of *smetana*, the Russian word for sour cream.

**SMITHFIELD HAM**—A special type of ham from the meat of hogs cured, smoked, and aged in Smithfield, Virginia, at the mouth of the James River.

Historically, Smithfield hams have always enjoyed an international reputation. England's Queen Victoria had these hams shipped to her, and both Sarah Bernhardt and Germany's Kaiser William rated the Smithfield ham far above any delicacy of their own cuisine. Reportedly, gourmand Diamond Jim Brady ate entire Smithfield hams in just one meal.

It was an Englishman, Mallory Todd, who set into motion the Smithfield ham industry. He set up a curing plant and smokehouse near the present-day site.

Dry salt curing and dehydration are the basic principles involved in the production of the famous Smithfield hams. The hams are first covered with salt and a curing agent. As the salt penetrates the ham, some of the natural juice is drawn out. Before smoking, hams are coated with

Recognize famous Smithfield hams by their coarse black pepper coating. The rich, lean meat should be served in paper-thin slices.

ground pepper for protection from insects. The dehydration process during the aging period continues for at least six months and may go as long as one and one-half years. The tenderness of the aged ham is believed to be caused, in part, by the protein breakdown during aging.

Directions for ham preparation are in the cloth bag used to cover the meat. The ham is usually soaked for 24 to 48 hours, washed and scraped, simmered in water, skinned, and glazed if desired. It is best sliced and panfried or baked whole then served thinly sliced. (See also *Ham*.)

**SMOKE COOKER**—Equipment specially designed so that the food hangs in a chamber away from the direct heat of the fire and is cooked by hot smoke. Originally a Chinese apparatus, the cooker has a chimney at one end of the firebox in which the food is hung from hooks. Openings at the top of the chimney and at the firebox opening control the draft. The cooking chamber fills with hot smoke as the wood chips burn in the firebox. Smoke cooking imparts a special flavor to the meat, depending upon the type of wood. (See also *Barbecue*.)

**SMOKE COOKERY**—A method of outdoor cookery in which the food is cooked by hot smoke in a smoke cooker instead of directly over hot coals. (See also *Barbecue*.)

**SMOKED FISH**—Fish that has been exposed to smoke from hardwoods, in the presence of low heat, until the flavor of smoke has penetrated throughout the fish. Undoubtedly man learned thousands of years ago that by stringing the fish on a stick over the fire he obtained a good, smoky taste and was able to store the fish for a long time. The commercial smoking of fish is a controlled process.

It essentially involves hanging the fish above the smoke of a dampened wood fire for a specified length of time. The fish is generally cured in a brine solution before it is smoked. During the smoking process, the fish absorbs the aroma of the smoke, which depends upon the particular type of wood that is used. Hickory is the most popular wood, but other hardwoods such as maple are also used.

Fish are smoked both whole or in pieces. Whole fish are drawn before they are smoked, while some large fish are cut into steaks or chunks. The whole process—splitting, cleaning, salting, drying, and smoking such fish as herring or salmon—is commonly known as kippering.

You will find some smoked fish by the pieces or sliced to order in fish markets and delicatessens. They are also available in cans or packages.

Look for these popular kinds of smoked fish: anchovy, bloaters or herring, butterfish, carp, chub, black cod, eel, finnan haddie, haddock, halibut, kippers, mackerel, salmon (lox), sardine, shad, sturgeon, trout, and whitefish.

While smoked fish need not be cooked before eating, you may cook them if you wish. Panfried or poached bloaters, for example, make a good breakfast dish. Finnan haddie or smoked haddock is delicious broiled and served with a sauce, or baked in milk. Smoked salmon or halibut makes a hearty casserole with rice and seasonings. Smoked whitefish or chub is a good lunch dish with potato salad and tomatoes.

Smoked eel, thin slices of smoked sturgeon or salmon, and smoked anchovies are tasty appetizer foods. Serve with crackers or rye bread slices. (See also *Fish*.)

## Smoked Salmon and Macaroni

**1 3⅔-ounce can sliced, smoked salmon**
**1 15-ounce can macaroni and cheese**
**1 3-ounce can chopped mushrooms, drained**
**¼ cup chopped green pepper**
**1 teaspoon instant minced onion**
**3 hard-cooked eggs, chopped**
**2 tablespoons butter or margarine**
**1½ cups soft bread crumbs**

Rinse, drain, and cut salmon into small pieces. Combine all ingredients *except butter and crumbs*. Turn into a 1-quart casserole. Melt butter; toss with crumbs. Sprinkle over casserole. Bake, uncovered, at 350° for 30 to 35 minutes. Garnish with green pepper rings or hard-cooked egg slices, if desired. Serves 3 or 4.

## Smoked Eel Canapés

**6 thin slices party pumpernickel**
**Butter or margarine**
**12 thin slices skinned, smoked eel or other dry, smoked fish (about one 4-ounce fish)**
**1/4 cup dairy sour cream**
**1 teaspoon finely chopped onion**
**Capers, drained**

Spread bread slices with butter or margarine; cut each slice of bread in half. Lay one slice fish atop each half. Combine sour cream and onion. Spoon a dollop over smoked fish; garnish with capers. Makes 12 appetizers.

**SMOKED MEAT**—Meat that is cured by exposing it to smoke in the presence of low heat. Like smoked fish, the meat is hung above the smoke for a specified length of time until the flavor of smoke has penetrated throughout the meat. In commercial smoking of meat, special care is taken to ensure that the meat is not too dry after smoking, that the smoke is circulated properly for even penetration, and that the degree of smoke is just right for the specific meat product. Hickory is the traditional smoking wood, but other hardwoods, including maple, apple, and cherry, also are popular for preparing smoked meat.

More cuts of pork than any other type

Use a handy dry soup mix and prepared frozen patty shells to make Smoked Beef Luncheon. Bits of smoked, sliced beef are in the sauce. Spiced Peaches makes a delicious accompaniment.

of meat are smoked. People have learned to enjoy the flavor of pork and smoke together. It's the smoking after the meat curing that makes ham and bacon taste so different from the flavor of fresh or cured (pickled) pork.

Many sausages made of all pork or a mixture of meats, are smoked to add flavor and keeping quality. Some of these sausages require cooking before eating while others are safe for immediate eating.

A small amount of beef is cured and smoked. Smoked sliced beef differs from dried beef, though they look alike. Smoked sliced beef is made from coarsely ground beef formed into round or square logs that are cured, cooked, and smoked. Breakfast beef (erroneously called beef bacon) is another smoked beef product, packaged in slices that resemble bacon in size, but they are much more lean.

Birds, too, are smoked for good eating. But the small supply of smoked turkey, duckling, goose, and pheasant that comes to the market is very much in the luxury food category. Both smoked turkey and smoked pheasant are made into a pâté and canned, to use as an appetizer spread.

You can add smoke flavor to meats when you cook them over heat on a grill or rotisserie. Or you can brush liquid smoke on oven-cooked meats or sprinkle them with smoke-flavored seasoning.

As with fresh meats, a meat thermometer is best to test doneness of smoked meat.

Smoking does not change the nutritional value of meats. They are as good sources of protein, the B vitamins, and minerals after smoking as before.

## Smoked Beef Luncheon

**6 frozen patty shells**
**1 envelope leek soup mix**
**1¾ cups water**
**1 6-ounce can evaporated milk (⅔ cup)**
**3 drops bottled hot pepper sauce**
**1 3-ounce package smoked, sliced beef, coarsely snipped**
**2 tablespoons chopped, canned pimiento**
**Spiced Peaches**

Bake patty shells according to package directions. Prepare soup according to package directions, using the water and evaporated milk as the liquid. Stir in hot pepper sauce, beef, and pimiento; cook and stir till thick and bubbly. Spoon into patty shells. Serves 6.

*Spiced Peaches:* Heat canned peach halves for 5 minutes in syrup with stick cinnamon, a few whole cloves, and a dash of vinegar.

**SMOKE POINT**—The temperature at which heated fat starts to break down, giving off smoky vapor, and taking on an acrid flavor. The smoking point determines whether a fat is a suitable one to use for frying. Olive oil and butter have low smoking points and can only be used for panfrying or sautéeing with careful temperature control to make sure they do not overheat. Vegetable oils and shortening are the choices for deep-fat frying, for they can withstand high frying temperatures without breaking down. (See also *Fat*.)

**SMORGASBORD** ***(smôr' guhs bōrd', -bôrd')*** —A Swedish style luncheon or dinner buffet at which a variety of foods is offered. Smorgasbords are now very popular in the United States and other countries. (See also *Scandinavian Cookery*.)

**SMORREBROD** ***(smoe' ruh broeth)*** — The name for the tiny, open-face sandwiches of Denmark. (See also *Scandinavian Cookery*.)

**SMOTHER**—To cook food in a tightly covered container or massed together in their own juices or in a small amount of liquid.

**SMYRNA FIG** ***(smûr' nuh)***—A yellowish or greenish fig native to the Near East.

Smyrna fig cuttings, ancestors of California-grown Calimyrna figs, were brought to the United States in 1880. Although the trees thrived, the fruit from the trees did not develop properly until 1899 when the unique cross-pollination process of this fig type was discovered and could be put to use commercially. (See also *Fig*.)

**SNACK**—A small amount of food eaten at any time other than at mealtime. Sandwiches, fruits, and sweets are snacks.

**SNAIL**—A small mollusk with a one-part, spiral shell. Market-sized snails usually measure about 1 to 1½ inches in diameter. They feed on green plants and move by means of a muscular foot. They frequently are referred to as escargots on menus.

Snails live either in water or on land. The water type, usually smaller than the land ones, are found in Europe and the east coast of America, and are called periwinkles. Land snails live in France, Switzerland, Japan, Italy, and the middle United States. Some are caught wild and some are raised on farms. These are the ones most used as food; however, land and water snail are used interchangeably.

You can purchase fresh, canned, and frozen snails. Cook fresh ones immediately. First, soak them in warm water till they emerge from the shell. (Those that do not emerge should be discarded.) Then boil them in salted water of court bouillon. Afterwards rinse the snails and shells. Canned snails and shells can be bought together or separately. Both canned and frozen ones are ready to use.

Cook snails by frying, making into a sauce, or putting into the shells with a seasoned butter and baking. There are special plates designed to use when baking in shells. These have indentions so the shells will not slide or move on the tray.

When you are eating snails from the shell, use pincers or snail tongs and a small fork, such as a snail or oyster fork. Place the tongs, in the left hand, to hold the shell steady while you remove the snail with the fork. Then, eat the snail. Delicious. Do not waste the snail butter. Pour it onto the plate and dip French bread into the tasty mixture.

**SNAP BEAN**—A green or yellow-podded kidney bean eaten with the pod. The green varieties are called green beans; the yellow varieties, wax beans. When bent in half, fresh beans snap crisply. (See also *Bean.*)

**SNAPPER**—A group of large fish that live in warmer ocean areas. The red snapper is one of the best known. The gray snapper, muttonfish, schoolmaster, and yellowtail are also included as members of the snapper family. (See also *Red Snapper.*)

Use kitchen shears to snip foods, such as candied ginger, dates, parsley, or chives. Snip the food in small, uniform pieces.

**SNICKERDOODLE**—A spiced, shaped cookie. Often rolled in a cinnamon-sugar mixture, they may contain fruit. (See also *Cookie.*)

## Snickerdoodles

**½ cup shortening**
**½ cup butter or margarine**
**1½ cups sugar**
**2 eggs**
**2¾ cups sifted all-purpose flour**
**2 teaspoons cream of tartar**
**1 teaspoon baking soda**
**¼ teaspoon salt**
**3 tablespoons sugar**
**3 teaspoons ground cinnamon**

Cream together first 3 ingredients. Add eggs; beat till fluffy. Sift together flour, cream of tartar, baking soda, and salt; stir into creamed mixture. Shape into balls the size of small walnuts. Mix 3 tablespoons sugar and cinnamon; roll balls in sugar mixture. Place on *ungreased* baking sheet 2 inches apart. Bake at 400° for 10 to 12 minutes. Makes 7 dozen.

**SNIP**—To cut a food, such as parsley or chives, into little bits by clipping with quick, short strokes of scissors or shears.

**SNIPE**—A small game bird related to the woodcock. Although more slender than the woodcock, the snipe has a similar long, slender bill used for probing in the mud for food. The bird is most often cooked whole in a casserole or stuffed for roasting.

**SNOW**—A lovely refrigerator dessert made with stiffly beaten egg whites, gelatin, sugar, and fruit pulp or juice. Snow Pudding is an example. (See also *Dessert*.)

## Pineapple Fluff

*A delicate dessert to complete the menu—*

**1 20-ounce can crushed pineapple (juice pack)**
**1 envelope unflavored gelatin (1 tablespoon)**
**¼ cup sugar**
**¼ teaspoon salt**
. . .
**2 unbeaten egg whites**
**3 to 4 drops yellow food coloring**

Drain pineapple, reserving juice; add water to reserved pineapple juice to make 1½ cups. In medium saucepan combine gelatin, sugar, and salt; add the reserved pineapple juice mixture. Stir over low heat till gelatin and sugar dissolve. Remove from heat; chill in the refrigerator till mixture is partially set.

Turn into large mixer bowl; add egg whites and yellow food coloring. Beat at high speed with electric mixer till light and fluffy, about 5 minutes. Fold in pineapple and chill again till partially set. Turn into 5½-cup mold; chill. Unmold to serve. Makes 8 servings.

**SNOWBALL**—A round-shaped dessert such as cookie, cake, or ice cream which has been rolled in confectioners' sugar or frosted with white frosting and rolled in coconut to give a snowball appearance. You can also cover snowballs with whipped cream and serve them with your favorite fruit or chocolate sauce.

**SNOW CRAB**—The name for a species of crab previously known as tanner or queen crab, which weighs less than the king crab.

**SNOW PEA**—A flat podded pea with underdeveloped seed that is eaten with the pod. It is common to oriental cooking and is also widely known by the name of Chinese pea pod. (See also *Chinese Pea Pod*.)

**SODA *(beverage)*—1.** A soft drink that consists of carbonated water, flavoring, and syrup, often referred to as soda pop. **2.** A soft drink made with ice cream. Often referred to as an ice cream soda, it is sometimes topped with whipped cream, cherries, and nuts. (See *Beverage, Ice Cream Soda* for additional information.)

**SODA *(leavening agent)***—The common name for sodium bicarbonate or baking soda. The crystalline salt is used in making baking powder. (See also *Baking Soda*.)

**SODA WATER**—A carbonated beverage that has been charged under pressure with carbon dioxide gas. Ironically, soda water, a nonalcoholic beverage, came about through experimental tests done on gas for the production of beer.

Initially sold in Philadelphia drug and perfume stores as a medicine, soda water now is used for a variety of purposes—as a beverage, as a beverage mixer, and as an ingredient in soft drinks.

Its popularity as a mixer stems from its ability to reduce the heat in water. This is brought about by the escaping gas. Furthermore, its bubbly, sparkling characteristic upon opening makes it a pleasant mixer for punches and some alcoholic drinks. It is one of the basic ingredients, along with fruit juice and syrup, in most commercial soft drinks.

**SODIUM BICARBONATE**—The chemical name that is used for baking soda or bicarbonate of soda. (See also *Baking Soda*.)

**SOFT DRINK**—Nonalcoholic carbonated beverages including soda pop, soda water, ginger ale, root beer, and some fruit drinks. It is called "soda" in some areas, "pop" in others, and "tonic" in still other areas. A number of fruit-flavored powders are on the market for making a type of soft drink at home. Soft drinks can be used either for making several glasses of beverage at one time or to provide the fruit flavor for a punch. (See also *Beverage.*)

**SOFT-SHELL CLAM**—A type of clam that is found along the Atlantic coast from Chesapeake Bay to the Arctic Ocean. This clam differs from the hard and surf clams in that its shell is oval and thin. The clam's long neck, or siphon, prevents the shell from closing completely.

These clams can be eaten raw, but are usually steamed. In fact, they are often called "steamers." (See also *Clam.*)

**SOFT-SHELL CRAB**—A crab that has shed its hard shell during molting. The new shell, not yet hardened, is delightful when eaten with the crab meat. Soft-shell crabs that are sold in markets are usually blue crabs. (See also *Crab.*)

**SOFT WHEAT**—Any of several varieties of wheat low in gluten, including red winter and white wheat. Also known as pastry wheats, their flour is used in cakes, cookies, piecrusts, doughnuts, biscuits, and crackers. Soft white wheat is also used in breakfast cereals. (See also *Wheat.*)

**SOLE**—A saltwater or brackish water flatfish. A relative to the flounder, this fish has a flattened body, brown to gray coloring, black markings, and a small mouth. Both eyes are on the right side and the teeth are on the left or blind side. The flesh is white, firm, and delicately flavored.

The sole from the European coasts are of excellent quality, but the American ones are small and bony. Imported sole available in American markets is labeled Channel, Dover, or English sole. The fillet of sole, lemon sole, and gray sole in markets and on menus usually comes from flounder rather than from a true sole.

Packages of sole fillets and whole fish are sold both fresh and frozen. Some are available breaded and stuffed. Cook this fish like other lean fish by boiling, steaming, or frying. Or bake or broil it. If you do the latter, add butter.

One serving of uncooked sole (3x3x⅜-inch) contains 68 calories. This fish supplies protein, minerals, and B vitamins to the diet. (See also *Flounder.*)

## Sole with Grapes

*Spoon creamy wine-based sauce with seedless green grapes over fish before serving—*

**1 pound fresh or frozen sole fillets or other fish fillets**
**1 cup dry sauterne**
**Salt**
**½ cup light cream**
**2 teaspoons cornstarch**
**¼ teaspoon salt**
**½ cup seedless green grapes, halved**

Thaw frozen fish. Cut into 3 or 4 portions. Place fillets in greased 10-inch skillet. Add wine. Bring to boiling; reduce heat and simmer, covered, till fish flakes easily when tested with a fork, about 4 to 8 minutes. Remove fish to platter; sprinkle with salt. Keep the fish warm in a slow oven. Strain the wine.

Return ⅓ cup wine to skillet. Blend together light cream, cornstarch, and salt. Stir into wine in skillet; cook and stir till thickened and bubbly. Add grapes; heat through. Spoon sauce over fillets. Serves 3 or 4.

## Sole-Shrimp Kettle

**1 pound fresh or frozen sole fillets or other fish fillets**
**1 large onion, thinly sliced**
**¼ cup butter or margarine**
**3 chicken bouillon cubes, crushed**
**4 cups hot water**
**2 tablespoons lemon juice**
**1 teaspoon salt**
**⅛ teaspoon white pepper**
**1 pound fresh or frozen shelled shrimp**
**2 medium tomatoes, peeled and chopped**
**1 tablespoon snipped chives**

Thaw frozen fillets. Cut fillets into 1-inch chunks. In large saucepan cook onion in butter till tender. Add fish, bouillon cubes, water, lemon juice, salt, pepper, shrimp, and tomatoes. Bring to boiling. Reduce heat and simmer till fish flakes easily when tested with a fork and shrimp turns pink, 2 to 3 minutes. Sprinkle top with snipped chives. Serves 8.

**SOLID-STATE**—A type of small, lightweight electronic control used in a variety of household appliances. The controls need no heating power or warm-up time, use little electricity, and are very rugged. For example, solid-state components are used for speed controls in blenders and mixers, giving an unlimited range of speeds.

**SORGHUM**—**1.** A canelike grass similar to corn used for food, forage, and syrup. **2.** A thick sweet syrup that is prepared from the juices of sweet sorghum.

Originating in Africa and Asia, sorghum was one of the first wild plants to be adapted for domestic use by man. The Egyptians grew sorghum before 2200 B.C., and the Chinese and Indians cultivated it several thousands of years ago.

This annual grows from three to fifteen feet tall and yields smaller, rounder grains than other cereals. The sorghum grasses are divided into four main types; broomcorn, grain, grass, and sugar. Broomcorn sorghum has a cluster of long branches, referred to as the brush, that is used for carpet and whisk brooms. Grain sorghums are used for livestock feed and in alcoholic beverages, oil, and starch. Grass sorghum is used for hay and pasture usage. The sweet juice that sugar sorghum or sorgo yields from its stalks is used in making a pungent syrup.

This thick, sweet syrup is quite often used as a substitute for molasses in recipes. The sorghum syrup is most common in the southeastern portion of the United States. (See also *Grain.*)

**SORREL** ***(sôr′ uhl, sor′-)***—A perennial herb of the buckwheat family with long, oblong leaves. Some varieties of sorrel are cultivated, while others grow wild in Asia, Europe, and North America.

The varieties differ from one another in the intensity of the sharp acid flavor of the leaves. The least mild variety, referred to as dock, has foot-long leaves which are added to green salads or used as a potherb. French sorrel, with its shield-shaped leaves, and sour dock or garden sorrel, the most acid of these varieties, are used in breads, vegetable dishes, and as meat accompaniments. You will also find that chopped sorrel in an egg and sour cream broth forms the base for the Jewish specialty chilled soup, *schav.*

Sorrel, marketed in bunches, is available in limited amounts during the summer and early fall in some eastern markets. Choose fresh, green clean leaves. Clean and store sorrel like lettuce.

Sorrel leaves contain high amounts of vitamin A with some calcium, phosphorous, and vitamin C. (See also *Herb.*)

**SOUFFLÉ** ***(sōō flā′, sōō′ flā)***—**1.** A baked egg dish, based on a thick sauce with puréed or chopped ingredients added, and made high and puffy with beaten egg whites. **2.** An unbaked egg dish, with a whipped gelatin base which is chilled and served as a light, airy dessert.

The true baked soufflés are a pleasure to the palate and delight to the eye when handled correctly. These include nonsweet soufflés for appetizer or accompaniments, main-dish soufflés with relatively hearty ingredients, and sweet soufflés for dessert.

Appetizer or accompaniment soufflés have similar ingredients to main-dish soufflés, with fewer such ingredients as meat or cheese. Appetizer soufflés can be served in small, individual soufflé or custard dishes as can main-dish soufflés.

Combinations of hearty and satisfying ingredients make main-dish soufflés a treat. Combine two or more food items and let your cooking creativity take over. Think of such combinations as liver and onions, mushrooms and chicken or turkey, spinach and ham, and cheese and bacon. Main-dish soufflés are an elegant way to use leftovers such as ham or chicken.

The sweet or dessert soufflés are made much in the same way as nonsweet soufflés, except sugar is added to the sauce. Select a flavoring ingredient, such as chocolate or vanilla, and combine with a puréed fruit, nuts, or liqueur. Replace the liquid ingredients with a fresh fruit juice or a combination of juice and liqueur.

***Basic preparation:*** A combination of procedures leads to a perfect soufflé. Some of these factors include: a smooth sauce base, perfectly beaten egg whites, correct beating equipment, proper preparation of mold, proper folding in of whites, and the correct baking temperature.

Begin by separating the egg yolks from the egg whites. Do this as you remove the eggs from the refrigerator when they are easiest to separate. Then, while you prepare the sauce base, let the egg whites stand in a clean, dry bowl. Take care that there is no trace of fat or egg yolk in the bowl. A speck of egg yolk has enough fat in it to keep the white from beating properly. In a clean bowl, the whites beat to a great volume, especially when the egg whites are at room temperature.

The sauce is made basically as you make any white sauce. Make sure it is very smooth before adding the puréed or chopped meats, cheese, or vegetables. Beat the egg yolks until thick and lemon-colored. Then, slowly add hot sauce to yolks, a little at a time, stirring constantly.

You can refrigerate the sauce mixture till ready to use, if desired. Just reheat sauce before folding in beaten egg whites.

The important thing to remember is that the success of the soufflé is largely dependent upon the stiffly beaten egg whites which expand during heating, thus making the soufflé rise. Your goal is to incorporate as much air as possible into the beaten egg whites. This is most satisfactorily achieved with a wire whip. Lift the eggs as you whip, using a down, up, and over action. An electric mixer or a rotary egg beater can also be used, as long as you remember this action. When using the electric mixer, use a rubber spatula to lift the egg whites. Most recipes call for stiffly beaten egg whites, which means beating the egg whites till the peaks stand up straight but are still moist and glossy.

While it's convenient to have a special soufflé dish, you can substitute with a casserole dish with straight sides. The soufflé dish, because it's made for this specialty, is best with its round shape and straight sides. Made of metal, porcelain, or glass, it ranges in size anywhere from one to eight cups. In any case, use the right size baking dish.

The soufflé climbs as it bakes, so collar the dish to keep it in bounds if you want the soufflé to rise above the dish. To do this, simply fasten a piece of buttered waxed paper around outside rim of the dish. A string or paper clip will hold it in place. Most soufflés climb best in an ungreased dish, but some do well in a buttered dish, often sprinkled with crumbs or sugar. However, follow recipe directions.

Folding the stiffly beaten egg whites into the base ingredients is the last preparation step. Before beginning, make sure you preheat the oven. This is very important for the best results are achieved in a well-regulated oven. Use a folding up and over motion, using a rubber spatula, when combining the egg whites with the base ingredients. Avoid mixing too thoroughly and perform the operation as quickly as

Trace a circle in soufflé mixture one inch from edge of dish and about one inch deep for a top hat that will puff in the oven.

Fasten a piece of buttered waxed paper around the outside rim of dish for an extra high soufflé. Secure with a string or clip.

possible. For a soufflé with a top hat that puffs in the oven, trace a circle through the mixture one inch from the edge and one inch deep.

Put the soufflé in the oven. You can forget about it till the end of the baking time. The length of the baking time often becomes a difference of opinion. The French prefer baking the soufflé in less time so it will have a soft runny center which may serve as a sauce for the firmer baked part. Americans prefer the soufflé baked completely throughout. Generally, you can test the doneness of a soufflé by inserting a knife off-center. The knife should come out clean. However, do not open oven door to peek, for drafts can damage the structure of the baked dish. Test doneness only at end of baking time.

***Serve soufflés immediately***

For the least amount of damage and to lessen the normal sinking of the soufflé, use two forks to break soufflé into servings. Then lightly spoon soufflé on individual plates. Pass an appropriate sauce or fruit garnish.

## Easy Cheese Soufflé

In saucepan combine one 11-ounce can condensed Cheddar cheese soup and 4 ounces process American cheese, shredded (1 cup). Cook and stir over low heat till cheese melts. Remove from heat. Beat 4 egg yolks till thick and lemon-colored. Slowly add cheese mixture to beaten egg yolks, stirring constantly. Fold cheese mixture into 4 stiffly beaten egg whites. Pour into *ungreased* 2-quart soufflé dish or casserole. Bake at 300° till knife inserted off-center comes out clean, about 1 hour. Serve immediately. Makes 4 to 6 servings.

***Elegant entertaining***

←Set an elegant mood with light and rich Turkey Soufflé served with Dilled Mushroom Sauce. Another time make it with chicken.

## Potato Puff Soufflé

**2 teaspoons minced onion**
**1/4 cup butter or margarine**
**1/4 cup all-purpose flour**
**1 teaspoon salt**
**Dash pepper**
**1 cup dairy sour cream**
**2 cups hot mashed potatoes**
**4 well-beaten egg yolks**
**4 stiffly beaten egg whites**

Cook onion in butter till tender. Blend in flour, salt, and pepper. Heat till bubbly. Remove from heat. Stir in sour cream and potatoes; beat smooth. Add small amount of hot mixture to egg yolks, stirring constantly. Return to hot mixture; mix well. Fold in whites. Pour into *ungreased* 1½-quart soufflé dish. Bake at 350° till knife inserted off-center comes out clean, 30 to 35 minutes. Serves 6.

## Spinach Soufflé

**1 10-ounce package frozen, chopped spinach**
**2 tablespoons butter or margarine**
**2 tablespoons all-purpose flour**
**1/2 teaspoon salt**
**1/2 cup milk**
**1/4 cup grated Parmesan cheese**
**5 egg yolks**
**5 stiffly beaten egg whites**
**Cheddar Cheese Sauce**

Cook spinach following package directions. Drain *very thoroughly.* Add butter to spinach; cook and stir over high heat till butter is melted. Blend in flour and salt; add milk all at once. Cook and stir over medium heat till mixture thickens and bubbles. Remove from heat; stir in grated Parmesan cheese.

Beat egg yolks till thick and lemon-colored. Stir spinach into egg yolks. Pour spinach mixture over egg whites; fold together carefully. Pour into an *ungreased* 1-quart soufflé dish. Bake at 350° till knife inserted off-center comes out clean, about 30 to 35 minutes. Makes 4 to 6 servings. Serve with Cheddar Cheese Sauce.

*Cheddar Cheese Sauce:* Combine one 10½-ounce can condensed cream of mushroom soup and ⅓ cup milk; heat. Add 4 ounces sharp natural Cheddar cheese, shredded (1 cup); stir.

## Macaroni Puff Soufflé

**½ cup elbow macaroni, cooked and drained**
**1 3-ounce can mushrooms, drained**
**1 cup milk**
**3 egg yolks**
**½ small onion, cut in pieces**
**3 tablespoons all-purpose flour**
**½ teaspoon salt**
**¼ small green pepper, cut in pieces**
**4 ounces sharp process American cheese, cut in cubes (1 cup)**
**3 egg whites**
**¼ teaspoon cream of tartar**

Place macaroni and water to cover in blender; blend till coarsely chopped. Drain. Pour macaroni into saucepan; add mushrooms. Place milk, egg yolks, onion, flour, and salt in blender container; blend smooth. Add green pepper and cheese; blend till coarsely chopped. Pour over macaroni. Cook and stir till thick and bubbly. Beat egg whites with cream of tartar till stiff peaks form. Fold into macaroni mixture. Bake in an *ungreased* 1½-quart soufflé dish at 325° till knife inserted off-center comes out clean, 50 to 55 minutes. Makes 6 servings.

## Crab Soufflé Bake

**3 tablespoons butter or margarine**
**3 tablespoons all-purpose flour**
**1 teaspoon salt**
**1 cup milk**
**3 eggs, separated**
**1 7½-ounce can crab meat, drained, flaked, and cartilage removed**
**1 3-ounce can chopped mushrooms, drained**

In a saucepan melt butter; blend in flour, salt, and dash pepper. Add milk. Cook and stir till thick and bubbly. Remove from heat. Beat egg yolks till thick and lemon-colored. Slowly add the sauce mixture to the egg yolks, stirring constantly. Stir in crab and mushrooms. Beat egg whites till stiff peaks form. Fold into crab mixture. Turn into an *ungreased* 1-quart soufflé dish. Bake at 325° till a knife inserted off-center comes out clean, about 60 minutes. Serve immediately. Makes 4 or 5 servings.

Pour gelatin-type soufflé into collared soufflé dish for chilling. Gently remove the waxed paper collar before serving.

## Turkey Soufflé

*Select turkey or chicken to make this elegant soufflé, and serve it with dilled mushroom sauce—*

In medium saucepan melt 3 tablespoons butter or margarine; blend in 3 tablespoons all-purpose flour, 1 teaspoon salt, dash pepper, and ¼ teaspoon paprika. Add 1 cup milk to mixture all at once. Cook quickly, stirring constantly, till mixture is thickened and bubbly. Remove from heat. Stir in 1 teaspoon grated onion, 1 cup finely chopped, cooked turkey or chicken, and 1 tablespoon snipped parsley.

Beat 3 egg yolks till thick and lemon-colored. *Slowly* add turkey mixture to egg yolks, stirring constantly. Cool slightly. Add gradually to 3 stiffly beaten egg whites, folding together thoroughly. Turn into *ungreased* 1 quart soufflé dish. Bake at 325° till knife inserted off-center comes out clean, 50 minutes. Serve with Dilled Mushroom Sauce. Makes 4 servings.

*Dilled Mushroom Sauce:* In saucepan cook 2 tablespoons chopped onion in 2 tablespoons butter or margarine till tender but not brown. Stir in 2 tablespoons all-purpose flour; ¼ teaspoon dried dillweed, crushed; ¼ teaspoon salt; dash pepper; and one 3-ounce can chopped mushrooms, drained. Add 1¼ cups milk to mixture all at once. Cook, stirring constantly, till mixture is thick and bubbly. Makes 1½ cups.

## Tuna Soufflé

- 1/4 cup butter or margarine
- 1/4 cup all-purpose flour
- 1/4 teaspoon salt
- 1 cup milk
- 4 ounces sharp process American cheese, shredded (1 cup)
- 1 6 1/2- or 7-ounce can tuna, drained and flaked
- 2 tablespoons chopped, canned pimiento
- 4 eggs, separated

In saucepan melt butter; blend in flour and salt. Add milk; cook and stir till mixture is thickened and bubbly. Remove from heat. Add cheese, tuna, and pimiento; stir till cheese melts. Beat egg yolks till thick and lemon-colored. Slowly add cheese mixture, stirring constantly; cool slightly. Wash beaters. Beat egg whites to stiff peaks. Gradually pour yolk mixture over whites, folding together.

Pour into *ungreased* 1 1/2-quart soufflé dish. For top hat that puffs, trace a circle through mixture 1 inch from edge and 1 inch deep. Bake at 300° till knife inserted off-center comes out clean, 65 to 70 minutes. Break apart into servings with two forks. Makes 4 servings.

## Chocolate Cloud Soufflé

- 1/3 cup light cream
- 1 3-ounce package cream cheese
- 1/2 cup semisweet chocolate pieces
- 3 egg yolks
- Dash salt
- 3 egg whites
- 1/4 cup sifted confectioners' sugar

In saucepan blend cream and cream cheese over very low heat. Add chocolate pieces; cook and stir till melted. Cool. Beat egg yolks with salt till thick and lemon-colored. Gradually blend into chocolate mixture. Beat egg whites till soft peaks form. Gradually add confectioners' sugar, beating till stiff peaks form. Fold a small amount of beaten egg white into chocolate mixture; carefully fold chocolate mixture, half at a time, into egg whites.

Pour into *ungreased* 1-quart soufflé dish. Bake at 300° till knife inserted off-center comes out clean, 50 minutes. Makes 5 or 6 servings.

The chilled soufflés, made with a whipped gelatin base, are almost foolproof and look much like a true soufflé. Pile the gelatin mixture in a collared soufflé dish and chill. (See also *Egg*.)

## Orange Dessert Soufflé

In saucepan combine 1/4 cup sugar, 1 envelope unflavored gelatin (1 tablespoon), and 1/8 teaspoon salt; add 1 1/2 cups cold water. Stir over low heat till dissolved. Stir small amount of hot mixture into 3 slightly beaten egg yolks; return egg mixture to saucepan. Cook and stir over low heat till mixture coats metal spoon, 2 to 3 minutes. Remove from heat; stir in 1/3 cup orange-flavored breakfast drink powder. Chill till partially set; stir occasionally.

Prepare one 2- or 2 1/8-ounce package dessert topping mixture according to package directions; fold the topping mix into the gelatin mixture. Beat 3 egg whites to soft peaks. Gradually add 1/4 cup sugar, beating the mixture till stiff peaks form. Fold into the gelatin mixture. Turn into a 5-cup soufflé dish with a foil collar. Chill till firm, 5 to 6 hours or overnight. Remove collar. If desired, garnish with chocolate curls. Makes 8 servings.

Relatively inexpensive, yet impressive, is Orange Dessert Soufflé prepared with flavored drink powder and dessert topping mix.

# SOUP

***Exciting ideas for nourishing soups, from clear broths to hearty chowders.***

When the familiar call from the kitchen is "soup's on," this could mean that any one of hundreds of soups is set on the table waiting to be eaten. Technically, a soup is usually defined as any liquid food in which a solid is cooked. Solids can be meat and/or bones, poultry, seafood, pasta, vegetables, or fruit. Because of such variety, soups can be hearty or thin, clear or thick, hot or cold. There is seemingly no end to the types and kinds of soups from which to choose.

Even the word "soup" has many derivations. Some say that it was named after the bread, referred to as sops, that was dipped into a liquid before being eaten. Others say it came from the sound that was made when soup was drunk from a cup.

Early souplike mixtures were often referred to as pottages. They were thick and generally were made of vegetables. One of the earliest written references is made in the *Holy Bible*. Esau, in the book of Genesis, sold his birthright for a pottage of lentils, a red lentil soup.

As time went on meat was added to the vegetable mixtures. Then, as the art of cooking developed still further—or perhaps out of necessity—clear, broth-type soups were introduced. Thinner soups were often prepared that way because of a lack of solid ingredients during times of food scarcities. In earlier days in the United States, a pot of soup stock was often found simmering on the back of the stove.

***Hearty soups to serve with crackers***

← Ladle out steaming bowlfuls of Ham and Pea Soup, Supper Corn Chowder, or Meatball Chowder for a chilly-day supper.

***Nutritional value:*** Soup is as nutritious as the ingredients that are used in the preparation. Hearty soup can play an important part in the daily diet for the entire family. Not only is it a source of liquid, which is a dietary necessity, but many soups furnish concentrated nutrients in a form easy to eat and digest. An example is soup prepared with milk, where you get the nutrients of the milk as well as the nutritional value of whatever other ingredients are used in the mixture.

In addition to being nutritious, soups have a wide range of caloric counts. Some are especially good for dieters. Soup is so filling that it should be planned in the calorie-counter's menu. A serving of chicken broth contains 11 calories, while beef broth has 23 calories. Other soups such as cream soups, chowders, bean and pea soups are among those that rank higher in calories. Regardless of the calories, soups can be used to vary the menu for dieters and nondieters alike. Everyone gains nutritionally from a bowl of soup.

## National favorites

Soupmaking plays an integral part in the cuisines of almost every country. Practically any food you can think of is used in soup somewhere in the world. In some cases the ingredients and flavors that are used will tell you quickly in which country a soup originated. In others, the combination of ingredients is somewhat startling. There are thin soups and there are those nearly as thick as stew, brimming with vegetables and meat.

American favorites include the seafood chowders of the coast, the gumbos of New Orleans, and the highly popular tomato soup. Although vichyssoise is an adapted

French peasant soup, it was invented by a chef of a New York hotel. This potato soup, flavored with leeks, is generally served cold. It has become an elegant soup, standard at gourmet dinners as the appetizer course. Another typically American soup is Philadelphia pepper pot, a well-seasoned mixture of tripe and vegetables, which was first put together in a steaming pot during the American revolution.

Favorites of European countries include the broths, onion soup, and bouillabaisse, a hearty seafood chowder of France. Pot au feu, which translated, means pot on the fire, is another French favorite—a rich meat-and-vegetable soup—derived from the peasants but universally popular.

Other foreign favorites include the oxtail and beer soups of Germany, minestrone of Italy, Spanish gazpacho, and the mulligatawny of India. Soups typical of other countries are the Scandinavian buttermilk soups and yellow split pea soup with pork, Russian cabbage soup and borsch, and the bird's nest soup and custard soup of China. A favorite Greek soup is a soup called avgolemono.

Some of these soups have been adapted to the modern kitchen and make use of timesaving appliances and convenience products which can be purchased.

## Blender Vichyssoise

**1 10¼-ounce can frozen condensed cream of potato soup**
**1 10½-ounce can condensed cream of chicken soup**
**1 soup can milk**

**. . .**

**1 cup light cream**
**Snipped chives**

In a saucepan heat frozen potato soup until thawed. Pour soup into a blender container. (Or use a mixing bowl.) Add cream of chicken soup and milk. Blend or beat till smooth.

Add light cream; blend a few additional seconds. Cover and chill thoroughly, 3 or 4 hours or overnight. (If desired, blend again just before serving.) Serve soup in chilled bowls or cups. Garnish each serving of soup with snipped chives. Makes 4 servings.

## Blender Gazpacho

**3 cups tomato juice**
**2 tablespoons olive *or* salad oil**
**2 tablespoons wine vinegar**
**1 clove garlic**
**2 medium tomatoes, peeled and quartered**
**1 small cucumber, cut in pieces**
**1 small green pepper, cut in pieces**
**3 medium stalks celery, sliced**
**¼ medium onion, cut in pieces**
**4 sprigs parsley**
**2 slices bread, torn in pieces**
**1 teaspoon salt**
**¼ teaspoon freshly ground pepper**
**1 cup croutons**
**Cucumber slices**

Put *1 cup* of the tomato juice, olive *or* salad oil, wine vinegar, and garlic in blender container. Blend till garlic is finely chopped.

Add *half each* of the tomato, cucumber, green pepper, celery, onion, parsley, bread, salt, and pepper to blender container. Blend till vegetables are pureed. Transfer to 2-quart container. Repeat with remaining tomato juice, vegetables, bread, and seasonings. Cover and chill. Serve in chilled mugs or bowls topped with croutons and cucumber slices. Serves 6.

## Speedy Borsch

**1 16-ounce can beets**
**2 10½-ounce cans condensed consommé**
**2 tablespoons lemon juice**

Drain beets, reserving liquid. Finely chop enough beets to make ⅔ cup. Combine beets, beet liquid, consomme, and lemon juice; chill. Stir just before serving; serve in chilled cups or bowls. If desired, top with dairy sour cream and snipped parsley. Makes 6 servings.

### *Festive soup from Spain*

Blender Gazpacho is a chilled mixture chock-full of vegetables and thickened with bread. Make it easily with an electric blender. →

## Types of soups

Because of the number of ingredients that go into the making of soups, there are a large variety of soups. The gamut is anywhere from clear appetizer soups to the heartier soups served as a main course, alone, or with bread or crackers.

The clear soups include stock, broth, bouillon, and consommé, while the heartier soups include cream soups, bisques, chowders, puréed soups, and gumbos.

Fruit soups are a category that fit neither into the clear nor hearty groups. These specialized soups are often served as the first or last course of the meal.

No matter what type of soup you make, it takes time to make good soup from scratch. You can hurry up your soupmaking by using canned or packaged soup products available on the supermarket shelves. These convenience products often make a suitable base for another soup of your own concoction, or are delicious products in themselves.

***Clear soups:*** While the three words, stock, broth, and bouillon are frequently used interchangeably, consommé is often set apart from the others.

A *stock* is basic to most types of clear soups. No doubt it gets its name from the kettle or stock pot that was kept on the old-time stoves ready for use. In the pot, and when used as an ingredient, the liquid was referred to as stock, but once ladled out and served, it was called a *broth.*

Essentially, stock is the liquid in which meat, fish, or vegetables are slowly cooked together, and it is usually the base for a soup, sauce, or gravy with other ingredients added. Use inexpensive cuts of meat and poultry, sometimes bones, and combine them with a liquid—generally cold water. Then bring the mixture slowly to a boil. Because the less tender cuts of meat are used, simmer the stock for a long period of time to extract the flavorful juices into the liquid.

The major types of stock include brown stock, made from meat, bones, and vegetables which have first been browned; white stock, made from unbrowned ingredients or from lighter colored meats such as veal or chicken; fish stock, prepared from trimmings of the fish; and meatless vegetable stock.

For shortcut cooking, canned broths are available. These ready-made convenience products include canned chicken and beef broth and lamb-flavored Scotch broth.

*Bouillon,* the French word for stock or broth, has come to mean a clarified, strained, and seasoned broth. Remove the fat, clarify the broth, and then skim and strain it. The result: A plain, clear soup.

If you want a well-flavored liquid—the familiar court bouillon—in which to poach fish and vegetables or for a soup base, cook cut up onion and carrots, spices, herbs, other seasonings, and wine, if desired, in the liquid. Then strain.

For a quick bouillon, dissolve chicken, beef, or vegetable cubes or granules in hot water or prepare bouillon with beef- or chicken-flavored base.

*Consommé* is different from the other clear soups in that the liquid is boiled down until reduced by half, thus intensifying the flavor. It, too, starts with stock or broth prepared from meat or poultry. When reduced still further, oftentimes consommé will gel by itself when chilled, especially when cooked with bones. Most canned consommés have gelatin added.

Consommé is one type of clear soup that is enjoyed either hot or cold. Pasta, rice, or finely cut vegetables are frequently added when it is served hot. When served cold, consommé is jellied and makes an ideal appetizer course for a heavy entrée.

### Herbed Tomato Broth

**1 10½-ounce can condensed beef broth**
**1 cup tomato juice**
**¼ teaspoon dried marjoram leaves, crushed**
**¼ teaspoon dried thyme leaves, crushed**
**1 tablespoon snipped parsley**

Combine beef broth, tomato juice, ¾ cup water, marjoram, and thyme. Heat to boiling. Reduce heat and simmer 2 minutes. Ladle into bowls. Garnish with parsley Makes 6 servings.

Serve Hot Sherried Consommé as an appetizer in a crystal glass. Pour hot soup over a silver spoon to prevent cracking of glass.

## Hot Sherried Consommé

**2 10½-ounce cans condensed consommé**
**6 tablespoons dry sherry**

In a saucepan combine consommé, 1⅓ cups water, and dry sherry. Heat through. Serve warm as an appetizer. Makes 6 to 8 servings.

***Hearty soups:*** As with the clear soups, there often is a fine distinction between the types of soups that are most generally served as the main course, or in small portions as the appetizer course of the meal. Hearty soups include cream soups, puréed soups, bisques, chowders, gumbos, and other meat, poultry, seafood, and vegetable soups of many kinds.

*Cream soups* come in thick and thin varieties. Thicken some with flour and actually begin with a basic thin white sauce recipe. Thicken others with egg yolk and cream, rice, or vegetables. Use milk or cream as the liquid, or substitute vegetable juice, puréed vegetables, or broth for part of the milk. An important step is to season adequately a cream soup, or it will taste bland. Do make sure that the sauce for a cream soup is velvety smooth, because it is worth the effort to avoid disconcerting lumps when you serve the soup to family or guests.

Common types of cream soups include tomato, mushroom, chicken, celery, corn, potato, asparagus, and cheese.

A *bisque* is actually a cream soup with a shellfish or vegetable purée added, and often there are bits of solid food as well. The word bisque is most frequently used in connection with shellfish; however, there are some familiar vegetable bisques, too, such as tomato bisque.

*Puréed soups* are similar to bisques or cream soups. The pulp of puréed vegetables acts as the thickening agent. Use fresh, canned, or dried vegetables for this type of soup. Speed the task of puréeing the vegetables into a smooth mixture with the aid of a food mill or blender. Familiar puréed soups include those prepared with peas, lentils, or beans.

*Chowders* are another type of hearty soup. Originally, chowders were primarily seafood mixtures, but now vegetable chowders, such as corn chowder and meat chowders, are also popular. A chowder contains solid ingredients. Familiar American-style fish chowders include the Manhattan and New England clam chowders.

*Gumbo,* the Creole-inspired New Orleans specialty, incorporates seafood, meat, or poultry, and vegetables in its unique combination. What makes this soup different from other types of soup is primarily the fact that it is thickened with okra or gumbo filé powder.

There are a number of other soups that are hearty enough to satisfy the hungriest of appetites. However, many of these soups don't fit into a special category. Many of the meat, poultry, fish, and vegetable soups are in this group. For example, old-fashioned vegetable soup could fit into the chowder category, but it seems to be in a class by itself.

Fruit soups are another group that stands alone. Prepare these soups by cooking fresh or dried fruit in water or wine. Sweeten and slightly thicken the mixture, then serve warm or cold for an appetizer or dessert.

## Blender Bean Soup

**1 pound dry navy beans**
**3 medium carrots, sliced**
**1 meaty ham bone**
**2 teaspoons salt**
**¼ teaspoon pepper**
**1 bay leaf**
**1 medium onion, cut in pieces**

Place about a *third* of the dry navy beans in blender container; blend till chopped. Remove. Repeat process till all beans are chopped. Place carrots in blender container; cover with water. Blend till coarsely chopped; drain.

Combine chopped beans, carrots, 2 quarts water, ham bone, salt, pepper, and bay leaf in large kettle or Dutch oven. Cover; simmer 3 hours, adding onion the last half hour. Remove ham bone and bay leaf. Add about a *third* of the bean mixture at a time to blender container. Blend at low speed till nearly smooth. Cut ham off bone; add ham to soup. Serves 8.

## Cheeseburger Chowder

**1 pound ground beef**
**½ cup finely chopped celery**
**¼ cup chopped onion**
**2 tablespoons chopped green pepper**
**3 tablespoons all-purpose flour**
**½ teaspoon salt**
**4 cups milk**
**1 tablespoon beef-flavored gravy base**
**4 ounces sharp natural Cheddar cheese, shredded (1 cup)**

Brown beef in saucepan. Add vegetables; cook till tender. Blend in flour and ½ teaspoon salt. Add milk and gravy base. Stir over low heat till bubbly. Add cheese; cook and stir just till cheese melts. Serves 4 to 6.

## Supper Corn Chowder

**1 medium onion, thinly sliced and separated into rings**
**3 tablespoons butter or margarine**
**2 cups cooked or canned whole kernel corn**
**1 cup diced, cooked potatoes**
**1 10½-ounce can condensed cream of chicken soup**
**2½ cups milk**
**1 teaspoon salt**
**Dash pepper**

In large saucepan cook onion in butter or margarine till lightly browned. Add corn, potatoes, soup, milk, salt, and pepper. Heat to boiling. Reduce heat and simmer a minute or two. Dash each serving with paprika and top with butter, if desired. Makes 6 servings.

## Vegetable-Beef Soup

**3 pounds beef shank**
**1 18-ounce can tomato juice**
**⅓ cup chopped onion**
**4 teaspoons salt**
**2 teaspoons Worcestershire sauce**
**¼ teaspoon chili powder**
**2 bay leaves**
**1 16-ounce can tomatoes**
**1 cup diced celery**
**1 8¾-ounce can whole kernel corn**
**1 cup sliced carrots**
**1 cup diced, peeled potatoes**
**1 10-ounce package frozen lima beans**

Combine meat, tomato juice, onion, salt, Worcestershire sauce, chili powder, bay leaves, and 6 cups water in soup kettle. Cover and simmer 2 hours. Cut meat from bones in large cubes; strain broth and skim off excess fat. Add meat and vegetables to broth; cover and simmer 1 hour. Makes 8 servings.

### *A nourishing entrée*

Chunks of ground beef, milk, and sharp Cheddar cheese all contribute to the heartiness of creamy, Cheeseburger Chowder. →

### Potato-Pea Potage

**1 10½-ounce can frozen condensed green pea with ham soup**
**1 10¼-ounce can frozen condensed cream of potato soup**
**1½ soup cans water**
**4 ounces sharp process American cheese, shredded (1 cup)**

In saucepan combine soups, water, and cheese. Heat, stirring occasionally. Serves 4.

## Uses in menu

Soups fit into the appetizer, main dish, or dessert course of the menu. Be sure to include them often when planning meals. Because of the varieties available, you're sure to find many that will be favorites. Perfect accompaniments are crackers.

Once you've decided on the soup, choose a garnish that will enhance both flavor and appearance. Some garnishes also add texture to an otherwise smooth soup.

Prepare Chicken-Vegetable Chowder (see *Bean* for recipe) at home, then take the hot soup along on a picnic in an insulated plastic ice bucket or wide-mouth vacuum container.

**Soup garnishes**

Choose one of the following garnishes to add texture and enhance the appearance of soups.

*For clear soups:* Thin lemon slices; snipped parsley or chives; tiny meatballs or dumplings; avocado slices; sliced hard-cooked egg.

*For cream soups:* Dairy sour cream; salted whipped cream; sliced, chopped, or slivered nuts; snipped parsley or chives; croutons; shredded cheese; popcorn; puffed cereal.

*For chowders and meat soups:* Thin lemon slices; frankfurter slices; snipped parsley; crumbled, crisp-cooked bacon; corn chips; oyster crackers; croutons; popcorn.

*For chilled soups:* Dairy sour cream; thin unpeeled cucumber slices; thin lemon wedges.

***As an appetizer:*** Start out the meal with a soup. Plan it in conjunction with the remainder of the meal so that it blends well, flavorwise. There should be no duplication of flavors in the various courses.

An appetizer soup should stimulate the appetite, not dull it. So, serve a light soup with a hearty entrée and a heartier type soup with a light main dish. Also remember that small bowls or cups of well-seasoned appetizer soups will be appreciated to start out a meal. Appealing appetizers include broths, bouillons, and consommés, as well as thin cream soups.

## Confetti Consommé

*Only 22 calories per serving—*

**2 10½-ounce cans condensed chicken broth**
**½ cup shredded carrot**
**¼ cup chopped green pepper**
**¼ cup finely chopped green onion**

In medium saucepan combine chicken broth, 1⅔ cups water, and vegetables. Heat to boiling. Serve hot. Makes 10 servings.

## Savory Tomato Soup

**¼ cup chopped celery**
**2 tablespoons chopped green onion**
**1 tablespoon butter or margarine**
**2 teaspoons all-purpose flour**
**1 8-ounce can stewed tomatoes**
**¼ cup dry white wine *or* water**
**1 chicken bouillon cube**
**2 slices crisp-cooked bacon**

Cook celery and onion in butter till tender but not brown. Blend in flour. Add 1 cup water and remaining ingredients, except bacon; cook and stir till slightly thick. Reduce heat; cook for 15 minutes, stirring occasionally. Garnish with crumbled bacon. Serves 2.

## Chilled Avo-Mato Soup

**2 avocados, pitted and peeled**
**½ cup dairy sour cream**

. . .

**3 medium tomatoes, peeled and finely chopped (2 cups)**
**1 10½-ounce can condensed beef broth**
**¼ cup finely snipped green onion**
**1 tablespoon lemon juice**
**Dash bottled hot pepper sauce**

Blend avocados and sour cream with electric blender. (Or sieve avocados; mix well with sour cream.) Stir in remaining ingredients and 1 teaspoon salt. Chill thoroughly. Trim with sour cream, if desired. Serves 4 to 6.

DINNER FOR TWO

*Savory Tomato Soup*
*Broiled Chicken Halves*
*Asparagus Spears*
*Cranberry Sauce* *Hard Rolls*
*Caramel Sundaes*
*Iced Tea*

## MENU

MAN-PLEASING SUPPER

*Golden Cheese Soup* — *Parsley Dumplings*
*Tossed Green Salad* — *French Dressing*
*Baked Apples*
*Coffee*

***As a main dish:*** Choose one of the heartier, nourishing soups when featuring it as the main part of the meal. A hearty soup is a good supper dish, needing only a salad, a breadstuff, and dessert to complete the meal. Any not-too-heavy soup goes perfectly with a complementary-flavored salad or sandwich for a quickie luncheon.

Remember to serve hot soups steaming and cold soups well chilled.

### Golden Cheese Soup

**1/3 cup chopped carrots**
**1/3 cup chopped celery**
**2 tablespoons chopped onion**
**3 tablespoons butter or margarine**
**1/4 cup all-purpose flour**
**2 cups milk**
**1 13 3/4-ounce can chicken broth**
**5 ounces sharp process American cheese, shredded (1 1/4 cups)**
**Dumplings**

Cook carrots, celery, and onion till tender in 1 cup boiling, salted water. Do not drain. Melt butter in Dutch oven; blend in flour. Add milk; cook, and stir till thick. Add broth, cheese, and vegetables with liquid. Stir over low heat till cheese melts. Drop dumplings into bubbling soup. Cover tightly; cook over low heat for 20 minutes.

*Dumplings:* Sift together 1 cup sifted all-purpose flour, 2 teaspoons baking powder, and 1/4 teaspoon salt. Add 2 tablespoons snipped parsley. Combine 1/2 cup milk and 2 tablespoons melted shortening. Add to dry ingredients all at once; stir just till moistened. Drop by teaspoons into soup. Serves 6.

### Meat and Vegetable Soup

**1 envelope dry onion soup mix**

• • •

**1 16-ounce can meatballs with gravy**
**1 16-ounce can cream-style corn**
**1 10 3/4-ounce can condensed tomato soup**

Prepare the onion soup mix according to package directions. Add meatballs with gravy, corn, and tomato soup; stir till blended. Heat through. Makes 6 to 8 servings.

### Cheesy-Asparagus Soup

**2 tablespoons butter or margarine**
**2 tablespoons all-purpose flour**
**1 teaspoon salt**
**Dash ground nutmeg**
**Dash pepper**
**3 cups milk**

• • •

**1 10-ounce package frozen, cut asparagus, cooked and drained**
**6 ounces natural Cheddar cheese, shredded (1 1/2 cups)**
**Paprika**
**Grated Parmesan cheese**

Melt butter and blend in flour, salt, nutmeg, and pepper. Add milk all at once. Cook, stirring constantly, till mixture thickens and bubbles. Cook 2 minutes longer. Add asparagus (cut any large pieces) and cheese; stir till cheese melts. Garnish with a sprinkling of paprika and Parmesan cheese. Makes 6 servings.

## MENU

QUICK-FIXING LUNCH

*Meat and Vegetable Soup*
*Melba Toast* or *Crackers*
*Pear and Cottage Cheese Salad*
*Assorted Cookies*
*Milk*

## Pacific Chowder

4 slices bacon
1/4 cup chopped onion
2 tablespoons chopped green pepper
1 10 1/4-ounce can frozen condensed cream of potato soup *or* 1 10 1/2-ounce can condensed cream of potato soup
2 cups milk
1 6 1/2- or 7-ounce can tuna, drained

Cook bacon; drain and crumble, reserving drippings. Cook onion and green pepper in 2 tablespoons drippings just till tender. Add soup, milk, and dash salt; heat to boiling. Break tuna in chunks; stir into soup with *half* the bacon. Heat. Dash with paprika, if desired, and trim with remaining bacon. Makes 4 servings.

## Shrimp Chowder

*Goes together in a jiffy—*

1/2 cup finely chopped onion
1 tablespoon butter or margarine
1 10 1/2-ounce can condensed cream of celery soup
1 10 3/4-ounce can condensed clam chowder
1 1/2 soup cans water
1 4 1/2-ounce can shrimp, drained
1 tablespoon snipped parsley

In saucepan cook onion in butter or margarine till tender but not brown. Blend in the celery soup, clam chowder, water, drained shrimp, and snipped parsley. Simmer over low heat to blend flavors, about 5 minutes. Serves 6.

Fix a kettle of hearty Meat and Vegetable Soup when lunch must be prepared in a jiffy. Convenience foods combine to make a soup that tastes like it's been simmered for hours.

## Ham and Pea Soup

**1 pound split green peas (2 cups)**
**1 ham bone**
**½ cup coarsely chopped onion**
**½ cup coarsely chopped carrot**
**½ cup coarsely chopped celery**
**2 sprigs parsley**
**1 clove garlic, minced**
**1 bay leaf**
**¼ teaspoon salt**
**⅛ teaspoon ground thyme**
**Dash pepper**
**2 13¾-ounce cans chicken broth (3½ cups)**
**1 cup diced, fully cooked ham**

In large kettle combine peas and 5 cups water; bring to boiling. Reduce heat and simmer, covered, 45 minutes. Add ham bone and remaining ingredients except diced ham. Simmer, covered, 1½ hours longer. Remove ham bone and bay leaf. Press vegetables and liquid through a coarse sieve, if desired; return to kettle. Add diced ham and heat to boiling. Serves 8.

## Meatball Chowder

**1 beaten egg**
**⅔ cup soft bread crumbs**
**¼ cup finely chopped onion**
**½ teaspoon Worcestershire sauce**
**½ pound ground beef**
**2 tablespoons salad oil**
**1 beef bouillon cube**
**1 cup coarsely chopped carrot**
**½ teaspoon seasoned salt**
**1 cup diced, peeled potato**
**2 10½-ounce cans condensed cream of chicken soup**
**2 soup cans milk (2⅔ cups)**
**1 16-ounce can cut green beans, drained**

Combine first 4 ingredients and ¼ teaspoon salt. Add meat; mix well. Shape into 24 meatballs. Brown in oil in large saucepan. Drain off excess fat. Add bouillon cube and 1 cup water; stir to dissolve cube. Add carrots and seasoned salt; cover and cook over low heat 5 minutes. Add potatoes; cook till vegetables are tender, about 10 to 15 minutes. Add soup; blend in milk and beans. Heat through. Serves 8.

## Chicken Soups

*Use the broth from a stewed chicken, canned chicken broth, or chicken bouillon cubes dissolved in water when the recipe calls for chicken broth—*

*Easy Chicken-Noodle Soup:* Cook 1 cup noodles in 3 cups chicken broth till tender. Serves 4.

*Chicken-Rice Soup:* Cook ½ cup rice in 3 cups chicken broth till rice is tender. Serves 4.

*Chicken-Curry Soup:* Mix one 10½-ounce can condensed cream of chicken soup, 1¼ cups milk, and ½ teaspoon curry powder; chill. Add 2 tablespoons snipped parsley. Serves 3 or 4.

*Chicken-Mushroom Soup:* Combine one 10½-ounce can condensed cream of chicken soup and one 10½-ounce can condensed cream of mushroom soup in a saucepan. Add 1 can water; heat to boiling. Makes 4 servings.

## Chili-Frank Soup

**1 cup chopped carrots**
**½ cup chopped celery**
**4 frankfurters, sliced**
**1 11½-ounce can condensed bean with bacon soup**
**1 11-ounce can condensed chili with beef soup**

Cook carrots and celery in 1½ cups water with ¼ teaspoon salt till tender, about 10 to 12 minutes. Add remaining ingredients. Heat through, about 10 minutes. Makes 4 servings.

## Devil's Chowder

**1 10½-ounce can condensed cream of celery soup**
**1 8¾-ounce can cream-style corn**
**1 2½-ounce can deviled ham**
**1 tablespoon instant minced onion**
**Dash paprika**
**Dash ground nutmeg**
**1 soup can milk**

Combine all ingredients except milk. Gradually stir in milk. Cook and stir till heated through. Makes 2 or 3 servings.

For a company luncheon, this not-too-heavy, chilled, Blender Broccoli Soup goes perfectly with dainty, toasty-warm sandwiches.

## Blender Broccoli Soup

**1 10-ounce package frozen, chopped broccoli, partially thawed**
**1½ cups milk**
**1 cup light cream**
**1 teaspoon instant minced onion**
**2 beef bouillon cubes**
**Dash ground nutmeg**
**¼ teaspoon salt**

Break broccoli in small chunks. Put into blender container with ½ *cup* of the milk. Blend till broccoli is very fine. Add remaining milk, other ingredients, ¼ teaspoon salt, and dash pepper. Blend till smooth, 45 to 60 seconds. Chill. If desired, trim with dairy sour cream and snipped chives. Makes 4 or 5 servings.

## MENU

COMPANY FOR DINNER

*Pork Roast*
*Parslied New Potatoes*
*Broccoli Spears*
*Sliced Tomato Salad*
*Swedish Fruit Soup*
*Coffee* *Milk*

***As a dessert:*** Serve soup for dessert for an interesting finale to the meal. The most familiar type of dessert soup is the Scandinavian fruit soup made with a blend of dried fruits, delicately spiced and sweetened, then slightly thickened.

## Swedish Fruit Soup

**1 11-ounce package mixed dried fruits (1¾ cups)**
**½ cup light raisins**
**3 to 4 inches stick cinnamon**
**1 medium, unpared orange, thinly sliced and halved**
**1 18-ounce can pineapple juice**
**½ cup currant jelly**
**¼ cup sugar**
**2 tablespoons quick-cooking tapioca**
**¼ teaspoon salt**

In a large saucepan combine mixed dried fruits, raisins, cinnamon, and 4 cups water. Bring to boiling; simmer, uncovered, till fruits are tender, about 30 minutes. Add remaining ingredients. Bring to a boil, cover; cook over low heat 15 minutes longer, stirring occasionally. Remove stick cinnamon. Serve warm or chilled. Makes 8 to 10 servings.

## Cherry Soup

**1 16-ounce can pitted dark sweet cherries**
**1 tablespoon sugar**
**2 teaspoons cornstarch**
**4 inches stick cinnamon**
**1 small piece lemon peel**
**½ cup orange juice**
**⅓ cup dry sherry**
**Dairy sour cream**

Drain cherries, reserving syrup. Finely chop cherries. Blend syrup with sugar and cornstarch in a saucepan. Add cinnamon, lemon peel, orange juice, and chopped cherries. Cook and stir over medium heat till mixture thickens and bubbles. Cook 1 minute longer. Remove from heat. Remove cinnamon and lemon peel. Stir in sherry. Serve warm or chilled garnished with a dollop of sour cream. Makes 4 servings.

**SOUR**—**1.** A tart or acid taste. It is one of the basic taste sensations and is associated with the taste of foods such as vinegar or lemon juice. **2.** A mixed, alcoholic beverage having a sour taste.

The ingredients of the beverage include liquor of some type; lemon or lime juice, usually lemon; sugar; and sometimes soda water. These ingredients are shaken with cracked ice, then strained into a sour glass. Generally this drink is garnished with an orange slice and maraschino cherry. The beverages are named after the type of liquor that is used in them, for example, whiskey sour or rum sour.

**SOUR CREAM**—A creamy, thick dairy product made tangy by the action of a culture on sweet cream. Most of the sour cream available is made from sweet, light cream and is referred to as dairy sour cream in recipes. The milk fat content of the light cream must be at least 18 percent. In many markets, sour half and half (a comparable product with less fat) is available. Imitation sour creams and packaged sour cream sauce mixes are also marketed.

Although sour cream has been used by cooks for centuries, this early product was similar to, but not exactly the same as the dairy product that homemakers can buy today. The first sour cream was probably discovered many centuries ago when the cream skimmed off milk became sour because of the lack of refrigeration. As a result of this discovery, ways were found to quickly use this soured product.

Through the years, people became accustomed to foods prepared with soured cream. They made the cream by setting a container of heavy, sweet cream on the back of the old-fashioned stove until it became thick and had an acid flavor. The exact degree of acidity (sourness) of these early products varied. Sometimes, it was very acid, at other times, it was mild.

With the introduction of milk pasteurization, however, this method could no longer be used, since the pasteurization process kills the bacteria that were originally used to sour the cream. Consequently, scientists had to discover a way to sour pasteurized cream. They did this by inoculating homogenized pasteurized cream with lactic acid culture, then letting it ripen under certain conditions. A constantly flavored sour cream is the result.

***Nutritional value:*** Dairy sour cream is a tasty, stimulating food product that carries the important nutrients of milk. In addition, the milk fat that it contains is easily digested by the body.

Caloriewise, a tablespoon of dairy sour cream adds about 30 calories to the diet. Sour cream made from half and half, a cream with only 10 to 12 percent milk fat, has slightly fewer calories. One tablespoon of this type of sour cream adds about 18 calories to the daily diet.

***How to store and use sour cream:*** Place sour cream purchased from the supermarket refrigerated case in the home refrigerator as soon as possible after purchase. For best quality, use sour cream within three or four days after purchase. Canned imitation sour cream and packaged mixes will keep much longer on the shelf. Once opened, some of these products also need to be kept under refrigeration.

The uses for sour cream are varied. It adds a tangy, gourmet flavor to appetizers, soups, sandwiches, salads, meat dishes, vegetables, baked foods, candies, and desserts. Use it in baking and cooking, or enjoy it as it comes from the carton.

Because of its milk fat content, sour cream adds richness to baked products. In fact, dairy sour cream can replace some of the fat and milk in recipes such as pancakes and biscuits. It also gives distinctive flavor to cakes and cookies.

When cooking with dairy sour cream, remember not to overheat or boil it. If sour cream is cooked at too high a temperature or held over heat too long, even at a low temperature, it will break down, giving a thin, curdled product. When this happens, the appearance will be less appealing, although the flavor will still be satisfactory. If possible, add sour cream at the end of cooking time. Then, just heat the mixture through, but do not boil.

When sour cream is added to canned condensed soups, or if flour is added to the sour cream in a sauce recipe, the sour cream will not separate or curdle.

Sour cream and mayonnaise are blended for the creamy base of Herb-Curry Dip. Crisp, raw vegetables make flavorful dippers.

Sour cream is a perfect ingredient for dips, spreads, salad dressings, frostings, and desserts. It gives tangy flavor to main dishes, such as stroganoff, and it can be incorporated into vegetable or meat sauces. Or, use sour cream alone as a garnish for soup or as a delicious baked potato topper. (See also *Dairy Sour Cream.*)

## Herb-Curry Dip

**1 cup mayonnaise**
**½ cup dairy sour cream**
**1 teaspoon mixed herbs, crushed**
**¼ teaspoon salt**
**⅛ teaspoon curry powder**
**1 tablespoon snipped parsley**
**1 tablespoon grated onion**
**1½ teaspoons lemon juice**
**½ teaspoon Worcestershire sauce**
**2 teaspoons capers, drained**

Blend all ingredients. Chill. Serve with carrots and/or celery sticks, and cauliflowerets.

## Creamy Onion Dip

**1½ cups dairy sour cream**
**2 tablespoons dry onion soup mix**
**½ cup crumbled blue cheese**
**⅓ cup chopped walnuts**

Blend sour cream and onion soup mix. Stir in blue cheese and nuts. Makes 2 cups.

## Sour Cream Potato Salad

**⅓ cup Italian salad dressing**
**7 medium potatoes, cooked in jackets, peeled, and sliced**
**¾ cup sliced celery**
**⅓ cup sliced green onion**
**4 hard-cooked eggs**
**1 cup mayonnaise**
**½ cup dairy sour cream**
**1½ teaspoons prepared horseradish mustard**
**Salt**
**Celery seed**

Pour Italian dressing over warm potatoes; chill 2 hours. Add celery and onion. Chop egg whites; add to potatoes. Sieve yolks; mix with mayonnaise, sour cream, and horseradish mustard. Fold into salad. Add salt and celery seed to taste. Chill 2 hours. Makes 8 servings.

## Swiss Apple Salad

**4 medium unpeeled apples, diced**
**1 cup diced Swiss cheese**
**½ cup diced celery**
**1 cup dairy sour cream**
**Dash salt**

Combine apples, cheese, celery, sour cream, and salt. Chill thoroughly. Serves 6 to 8.

## Avocado-Cream Dressing

Combine 1 medium avocado, peeled and mashed; ½ cup dairy sour cream; 2 tablespoons milk; 2 teaspoons lemon juice; ½ teaspoon salt; ¼ teaspoon dried chervil leaves, crushed; dash onion powder; and 3 drops bottled hot pepper sauce. Chill. Serve over lettuce. Makes 1 cup.

## Chicken Liver Stroganoff

**1 cup chopped onion**
**2 tablespoons butter or margarine**
**½ pound chicken livers, halved**
**1 3-ounce can broiled, sliced mushrooms, undrained**
**1 tablespoon paprika**
**1 cup dairy sour cream**
**2 cups hot cooked rice**

Cook onion in butter till tender but not brown. Add livers and mushrooms. Stir in paprika, ½ teaspoon salt, and dash pepper. Cover; cook over low heat till livers are tender, 8 to 10 minutes. Stir in sour cream. Heat, *but do not boil.* Serve over hot, cooked rice. Trim with snipped parsley, if desired. Serves 4.

## Sour Cream Burgers

Combine 1 cup dairy sour cream, ¼ cup finely chopped onion, 2 teaspoons Worcestershire sauce, 1 teaspoon salt, and dash pepper. Add 2 pounds ground beef; mix well. Shape into 8 patties. Broil 3 inches from heat 6 minutes. Turn, broil 4 to 6 minutes longer. Meanwhile, dissolve 2 beef bouillon cubes in ¼ cup boiling water. Stir in 1 cup dairy sour cream and 2 tablespoons snipped parsley. Heat, *but do not boil.* Place each patty on half of a toasted hamburger bun. Top with cream sauce. Serves 8.

## Two-Berry Parfaits

**1 10-ounce package frozen raspberries, thawed**
**¼ cup sugar**
**2 tablespoons cornstarch**
**2 cups fresh strawberries, sliced**
**2 teaspoons lemon juice**
**1 quart vanilla ice cream**
**1 cup dairy sour cream**

Drain raspberries; reserve syrup. Add water to syrup to make 1 cup. In saucepan combine sugar and cornstarch; stir in syrup. Add strawberries. Cook and stir over medium-high heat till thickened and bubbly. Stir in raspberries and lemon juice; chill. In parfait glasses layer ice cream, berry sauce, sour cream, and berry sauce. Repeat layers. Serves 6 to 8.

Two-Berry Parfaits combine a ruby raspberry-strawberry sauce, tangy sour cream, and vanilla ice cream in a layered beauty.

## Sour Cream-Choco Cake

**½ cup shortening**
**2 cups sifted cake flour**
**2 cups sugar**
**1 teaspoon baking soda**
**½ cup dairy sour cream**
**½ teaspoon vanilla**
**4 1-ounce squares unsweetened chocolate, melted and cooled**
**2 eggs**
**Seven-Minute Frosting (See *Frosting*)**

Place shortening in large bowl. Sift in flour, sugar, soda, and ½ teaspoon salt. Add sour cream, vanilla, and ⅔ cup water. Mix till flour is moistened. Beat vigorously 2 minutes, scraping bottom and sides of bowl. Add chocolate, eggs, and ⅓ cup water; beat 2 minutes.

Bake in 2 greased and lightly floured 9x1½-inch round cake pans at 350° till cake tests done, about 25 to 30 minutes. Cool 10 minutes; remove from pans. Cool; fill and frost the cake with Seven-Minute Frosting.

## Sour Cream Frosting

**1 6-ounce package semisweet chocolate pieces**
**1/4 cup butter or margarine**
**1/2 cup dairy sour cream**
**1 teaspoon vanilla**
**1/4 teaspoon salt**
**2 1/2 to 2 3/4 cups sifted confectioners' sugar**

Melt semisweet chocolate pieces and butter over *hot, not boiling,* water; remove from hot water and blend in sour cream, vanilla, and salt. Gradually add enough sifted confectioners' sugar for spreading consistency; beat well. Frosts tops and sides of two 9-inch layers or one 10-inch tube cake.

## Quick Apricot Pastries

Unroll 1 package refrigerated crescent rolls (8 rolls); pat into bottom of a buttered 13½x 8¾x1¾-inch baking dish. Spread with ½ cup apricot jam. Bake at 425° for 15 minutes. Remove from oven. Reduce heat to 325°. Combine 1 cup dairy sour cream, 1 beaten egg, 1 tablespoon sugar, and ½ teaspoon vanilla. Pour evenly over rolls; bake 5 to 6 minutes longer. Serve warm. Makes about 12 pastries.

Old-fashioned Sourdough Bread gets its flavor from the fermented starter batter that is saved from one baking to the next.

**SOURDOUGH**—Fermented dough used originally instead of yeast for making bread. Early prospectors and cowboy cooks kept a piece of sourdough from every baking to use as a "starter" for leavening the next batch. Not only was it used for bread, but it was also a prime ingredient for flapjacks and biscuits. The word became a nickname for the Alaskan prospector who usually included sourdough in his supplies.

You'll find that making sourdough bread is a relatively slow process, but the distinctive flavor of the bread renders it a big favorite of many people. In some areas of the United States, the starter for sourdough bread is available as also is the baked sourdough bread.

## Sourdough Bread

*To make Starter Batter:* Dissolve 1 package active dry yeast in ½ cup warm water. Stir in 2 cups lukewarm water, 2 cups sifted all-purpose flour, 1 tablespoon sugar, and 1 teaspoon salt. Beat till smooth. Let stand, uncovered, at room temperature for 3 to 5 days. Stir 2 or 3 times daily; cover at night. (Starter should have a "yeasty," not sour, smell.) Cover and refrigerate till ready to make bread.

*To make bread:* In large bowl soften 1 package active dry yeast in 1½ cups warm water (110°). Blend in *1 cup* Starter Batter, 2 teaspoons salt, and 2 teaspoons sugar. Add 3½ cups sifted all-purpose flour. Beat 3 to 4 minutes. Cover; let rise till double, about 1½ hours. Mix ½ teaspoon baking soda with 1½ cups sifted all-purpose flour; stir into dough. Add ¼ to ½ cup sifted all-purpose flour to make a stiff dough.

Turn out on lightly floured surface; knead 8 to 10 minutes. Divide dough in half; cover and let rest 10 minutes. Shape in 2 round or oval loaves. Place on lightly greased baking sheets. With sharp knife, make diagonal gashes across top. Let rise till double, about 1½ hours. Bake at 400° for 35 to 40 minutes. Brush tops of loaves with melted butter.

*To keep Starter:* Add ½ cup water, ½ cup sifted all-purpose flour, and 1 teaspoon sugar to leftover Starter Batter. Let stand till bubbly and well fermented—at least 1 day. Store in the refrigerator. If not used within 10 days, add 1 teaspoon sugar to the Starter Batter.

**SOUR MILK**—Milk that has been soured either naturally or artificially. Unpasteurized milk is the only type that will ferment and sour naturally. However, since most of the milk that is sold is pasteurized, a process that kills the natural bacteria that causes milk to sour, naturally sour milk is almost impossible to find. In fact, pasteurized milk has a tendency to spoil instead of becoming sour.

For use in recipes, you can make sour milk very easily. Just add enough fresh milk or diluted evaporated milk to one tablespoon of vinegar or lemon juice to make one measuring cup full. Then, let the mixture stand for about five minutes and use it as the recipe directs.

Buttermilk can be substituted easily for most of the recipes calling for sour milk as an ingredient. Buttermilk is readily available in almost any food market.

Baking soda is used as all or part of the leavening in baked foods made with sour milk. It gives off leavening gas when mixed with the mild acid in the milk. In fact, one-fourth teaspoon baking soda plus one-half cup sour milk has the leavening power equivalent to one teaspoon of baking powder. (See also *Milk*.)

**SOUR SALT**—Coarse citric acid crystals used in some types of cookery to give the food a pleasantly tart taste.

**SOURSOP**—A large, pear-shaped tropical fruit with white, slightly acid-tasting pulp and soft prickles on a green skin. This fruit is related to the custard apple. (See also *Custard Apple*.)

**SOYBEAN**—A pod-bearing, leguminous plant. There are hundreds of varieties of soybeans with at least as many uses, including industrial as well as food products.

The soybean is native to Eastern Asia. Chinese records dating back to 2207 B.C. show that soybeans were among the first crops cultivated. The Chinese considered them to be one of the five sacred grains, along with rice, wheat, barley, and millet, essential to Chinese civilization.

Although there had been earlier experiments with soybeans in America, the varieties introduced by the Perry Expedition on its return from Japan in 1854 launched the crop in the United States. Experimentation has been done since.

Noodlelike Spaetzle complements flavorful Seafood Kabobs (see *Kabob* for recipe). Accompany this entree with green beans.

Protein, fat, vitamins, and minerals are the major nutrients in soybeans. The protein of the soybean is more complete than most vegetable proteins, and similar to animal protein. The amino acid composition of soybeans is much like that of casein, the protein in milk. Thus, soy products are valuable to people in areas where meat is not easily accessible, and to people on restricted diets. For infants allergic to milk, a soy formula is an alternative.

There are other uses for soybeans. Fresh soybean sprouts are used in Oriental cooking, and on the American table, soybeans are used as a green vegetable. The dried soybeans are baked or boiled much the same as navy beans. Probably the soy product most familiar to American homemakers, is soy sauce although there are many other uses of the vegetable.

In 1911, a Seattle mill first pressed oil from the soybean. Since that time, soybean oil has worked miraculous changes in the food industry by producing shortening, margarine, cooking oil, pastas, ice "cream," whipped toppings, and more.

Soy flour or meal is another valuable product that is rich in nutrients. Current research indicates that soy products can provide an effective weapon in the battle against world hunger.

**SOY FLOUR**—A flour milled from soybeans. It is not a new product since a soy flour was combined with water to make a substitute milk even before the Christian era.

Because soy protein so closely resembles animal protein, products made with soy flour provide an economical meat substitute. Since there is no gluten in this type of flour, it cannot successfully be used alone in baked products.

Products with the appearance and taste of meat are being made from defatted soy flours in a promising development.

**SOY SAUCE**—A salty, fermented sauce of soybeans, water, and salt. Soy sauce is an essential ingredient in Oriental cookery. It adds both salty flavor as well as its typically brown color and is used in such dishes as chow mein and chop suey.

Japanese call their soy sauce *shoyu.* Flavorwise, it is between the light and dark Chinese soy sauce. American homemakers can usually find both soy sauce and *shoyu* in their local supermarkets.

Its use is not limited, however, to oriental cooking. Soy sauce has become a popular ingredient in barbecue sauces, other meat dishes, and marinades. And it is an ingredient in the popular teriyaki dishes. (See also *Oriental Cookery.*)

## Lamb Chops Oriental

**6 shoulder lamb chops, ¾ inch thick**
**½ cup soy sauce**
**½ cup water**
**1 clove garlic, minced**

Slash fat edges of chops. Place in shallow baking dish. Combine soy sauce, water, and garlic; pour over chops. Cover; refrigerate several hours, turning once. Place the chops on the rack of the broiler pan; broil 3 inches from heat about 10 minutes. Turn chops and broil 5 to 8 minutes longer. Makes 6 servings.

## Teriyaki Burgers

Combine 2 beaten eggs; ¼ cup water; 3 tablespoons soy sauce; 1½ cups soft bread crumbs (2 slices); ¼ cup chopped onion; 2 tablespoons sugar; 1 small clove garlic, crushed; and dash ground ginger. Add 1½ pounds ground beef and mix well. Shape the mixture into 6 patties. Broil 4 to 5 inches from heat for 10 minutes, turning once. Makes 6 burgers.

**SPAETZLE, SPATZLE** ***(shpet′ sluh, -slē)***—A noodle or dumpling made from batter that is pressed through a colander, and cooked in boiling liquid. Spaetzle originated in Germany but is enjoyed in the cuisines of other countries as an accompaniment to meat dishes or in soups.

## Spaetzle

Sift together 2 cups sifted all-purpose flour and 1 teaspoon salt. Add 2 slightly beaten eggs and 1 cup milk; beat well. Place mixture in a coarse-sieved colander. Hold over large kettle of rapidly boiling, salted water. With wooden spoon, press batter through colander. Cook and stir 5 minutes; drain thoroughly. Serve as a meat accompaniment. Makes 5 servings.

Use a wooden spoon to press the Spaetzle batter through a colander into the kettle of boiling water. Drain noodles thoroughly.

**SPAGHETTI**—Pasta in slender, solid, rod form, or in elbow form. Like the other pastas—macaroni and noodles—spaghetti is made from a flour and wheat dough.

In America, "spaghetti" usually refers to spaghetti and sauce. This is popular family fare because it is filling, low in cost and when purchased ready-prepared (canned or frozen), is a time- and work-saver, too. However, there are many variations on "spaghetti," and given fancy toppings, it becomes a far cry from mother's favorite washday special.

Where spaghetti and other pasta forms originated is a matter for some dispute. Because Marco Polo is a well remembered figure, the story has persisted that he brought spaghetti back to Italy from the Orient. Another group insists that Italy is the cradle of pasta. They cite, among other things, a cook book by an anonymous author which is said to be the first published record of pasta. The publication date of this book predates Polo's trips by several years, so the Italians seem to have a strong case. To promote it, they have established a Spaghetti Museum in Pontedassio near the Italian Riviera.

Another legend claims that a group of invading Mongols brought pasta to Germany in the thirteenth century and from there it found its way to Italy.

While the true birthplace of pasta is not established, its use seems to have spread in the thirteenth century, although ancient documents show its existence in the Orient as early as 5000 B.C.

Whether pasta is native to Italy or not, there is no doubt that pastamaking matured to a fine art as a result of the inventive Italian cooks. The creative upsurge of the Renaissance was reflected in pasta manufacture by the development of myriad pasta shapes and recipes.

Commercial production of pasta was begun in Naples during the Renaissance and by the late fifteenth century, pasta had become the mainstay of the Italian menu. It was during these early periods that cooking itself became highly refined in Italy. Today, Italy is one country that still retains a solid reputation for artful cooking, due in part to its creative development of all types of pasta cookery.

Spaghetti was introduced to the United States by Thomas Jefferson. He brought a spaghetti die back from a trip to Italy in 1786. However, there is a long gap between this date and the actual commercial production of spaghetti in America. This is because the needed wheat variety, durum, was not grown here until many years later. It was first brought to North America in 1853. Then, in 1900, Dr. Mark A. Carleton, a wheat scientist with the United States Department of Agriculture, brought durum varieties from Russia that could successfully be grown in this country.

***How spaghetti is made:*** The flour used in pasta manufacture is usually from durum, a hard, amber-colored spring wheat. The durum flour produces pasta that retains firmness after it is cooked.

For pasta products like spaghetti, durum wheat is milled into a golden, granular product called "semolina." The semolina is mixed with water and kneaded into a soft dough that is forced through a die (pierced metal plate) into long strands. As the spaghetti emerges, a rack moves against it. A knife cuts the strands and these strands move on racks into driers or dehydration chambers. Spaghetti is not baked, but filtered air passes over it until it is dried. After drying, it is cut to exact lengths, weighed, and packaged.

***Nutritional value:*** Children rarely have to be coaxed to finish their spaghetti especially when flavorfully sauced. That is why the nutritional story of spaghetti is so reassuring to mothers. Enriched spaghetti contributes the B vitamins, thiamine, riboflavin, and niacin to the diet, in addition to some iron and protein. Meatballs, which often accompany spaghetti, contribute additional nutrients to the diet.

The calorie news is good, too. A one-cup serving of spaghetti adds up to just about 160 calories. The sauce or meat that usually are served with the pasta will add more calories, but it is the size of the serving that really determines the total calorie tally. In average servings, spaghetti is an aid to weight watchers, as it contributes to a feeling of fullness and lessens the likelihood of overeating.

To avoid breaking up spaghetti, hold handful at one end and dip other end into water. Curl it around in pan as it softens.

***Types of spaghetti:*** While the most familiar spaghetti is the straight, long rod, there are variations. There are even different thicknesses of the long rod which are each separately named—regular spaghetti; somewhat thinner spaghetti, called spaghettini; and nested vermicelli, which looks like a thick skein of delicate strands, or vermicelli in long, straight rods.

Other variations include elbow spaghetti; capellini and fedelini, very thin folded spaghetti; fusilli, which has a zigzag crimp; and tortiglioni, which comes in a spiral shape. Spaghetti à la chitarra is another variety that is named for its resemblance to guitar strings.

The shape has little effect on the flavor of the finished dish, but can add greatly to its eye appeal. Because there are so many interesting possibilities with spaghetti, the adventuresome cook will find it rewarding to experiment with new recipes. If a certain spaghetti variety is called for that the local market can't supply, another spaghetti of similar size usually can be substituted by weight.

***How to select and store:*** The most common spaghetti package sizes are 7, 8, and 16 ounces. When buying, count on eight average or six hearty servings to a pound. Since spaghetti requires no refrigeration, it is a foresighted homemaker who keeps a good supply on hand. Campers like spaghetti for its ease of storage, too.

Once the package is opened, uncooked spaghetti can be stored in its original package if it closes tightly. Otherwise, it should be transferred to a container that has a tight-fitting lid or cover.

After cooking, store leftover spaghetti in the refrigerator for a day or two. It will keep up to six months in the freezer.

***How to prepare spaghetti:*** A large saucepan and a colander are good basic equipment for all pasta cookery. Also helpful is a slotted spoon to give the cooking pasta an occasional stir, especially at the beginning of the cooking period. It's also a useful piece of equipment to lift out samples for taste testing.

The recommended ratio of water to pasta is four quarts to a pound. Two tablespoons of salt is the right seasoning for this amount. A teaspoon of cooking oil added to the water will reduce splashing when the water boils, and it will prevent the pasta from sticking together.

Children may find it easier to eat the elbow spaghetti that is in shorter lengths. Adults, however, can manage the long strands of spaghetti and often find it a challenge. To keep the strands whole when cooking, hold the spaghetti at one end and immerse the other in the boiling water. As it softens, curl it into the pan until all is covered by the water.

Spaghetti should be cooked, uncovered, until it reaches a stage the Italians call "al dente," which means that it is tender to the tooth. Spaghetti that is too firm or has a starchy flavor is underdone. Taste testing can begin after the spaghetti has boiled about six minutes, but the exact cooking time depends upon the thickness of the product and individual preference. When it is done, spaghetti should be well drained in a colander so that no water is left to thin the sauce.

If spaghetti is to be used in a recipe that calls for further cooking, as in a baked casserole, reduce the cooking time by about one-third. The spaghetti will finish cooking in the oven.

The more varied the sauces that accompany spaghetti, the more interesting its personality becomes. Spaghetti is a natural with ground beef for skillet or casserole type dishes, and it is perfect as a base for other types of meat, such as veal cutlets. Seafood also combines quite well with spaghetti. (See also *Pasta*.)

## Clam-Mushroom Spaghetti

**1 6-ounce can tomato paste**
**1/4 cup chopped onion**
**1/4 cup chopped green pepper**
**1 clove garlic, crushed**
**1/2 to 3/4 teaspoon dried basil leaves, crushed**
**1/2 teaspoon dried oregano leaves, crushed**
**1/8 teaspoon pepper**
**2 7 1/2-ounce cans minced clams**
**1 3-ounce can sliced mushrooms**
**8 ounces spaghetti, cooked**

In saucepan combine first 7 ingredients, 1/2 teaspoon salt, and 1 cup water. Drain clams and mushrooms; reserve liquids. Add liquids to saucepan; set clams and mushrooms aside. Simmer mixture, uncovered, to desired thickness. Add clams and mushrooms; heat. Serve over drained spaghetti. Serves 4.

## Spaghetti Marina

*Shrimp and olives add special flavor—*

**8 ounces spaghetti**
**3 tablespoons butter or margarine**
**3 tablespoons all-purpose flour**
**1/2 teaspoon dried dillweed**
**1 3/4 cups milk**
**2 4 1/2-ounce cans shrimp, drained**
**1/4 cup sliced, pitted ripe olives**
**1 tablespoon snipped parsley**
**1 tablespoon lemon juice**

Cook spaghetti according to package directions. Drain. In saucepan melt butter; stir in flour, dillweed, and dash salt. Add milk; cook and stir till slightly thickened and bubbly. Add shrimp, olives, parsley, and lemon juice. Heat through. Serve over hot spaghetti. Serves 4 or 5.

## Baked Spaghetti

*Good to prepare when cooking for a crowd—*

**16 ounces spaghetti**
**4 pounds ground beef**
**2 large onions, chopped (2 cups)**
**1 large green pepper, chopped (1 cup)**
**2 teaspoons salt**
**2 10 1/2-ounce cans condensed cream of mushroom soup**
**4 10 1/2-ounce cans condensed tomato soup**
**1 quart milk**
**1 pound sharp process American cheese, shredded (4 cups)**

Break spaghetti into 3-inch lengths. Cook in large amount boiling, salted water; drain. In Dutch oven or kettle cook meat, onion, and green pepper until meat is browned. Sprinkle with salt. Gradually stir in soups, milk, and 2 *cups* of the cheese. Divide cooked spaghetti evenly between two 13x9x2-inch baking dishes. Into each pan stir half the soup-meat mixture. Sprinkle the remaining 2 cups cheese atop both. Bake, uncovered, at 350° till hot through, about 1 hour. Makes 20 servings.

All it takes is one large skillet to prepare easy Skillet Spaghetti. The spaghetti cooks till done in the simmering sauce.

## Skillet Spaghetti

**1 pound ground beef**
**1 6-ounce can tomato paste**
**1 18-ounce can tomato juice**
**1½ to 2 teaspoons chili powder**
**1 teaspoon garlic salt**
**1 teaspoon salt**
**1 teaspoon sugar**
**1 teaspoon dried oregano leaves, crushed**
**2 tablespoons instant minced onion**
**7 ounces uncooked spaghetti**

In a large skillet break up the ground beef. Add the remaining ingredients except the spaghetti. Stir in 3 cups water. Cover; bring to boiling. Reduce heat; simmer 30 minutes, stirring occasionally. Add the spaghetti; stir to separate strands. Simmer, covered, till spaghetti is tender, about 30 minutes longer, stirring frequently. Pass a shaker of Parmesan cheese, if desired. Makes 4 to 6 servings.

## Veal Parmesan with Spaghetti

**6 thin veal cutlets (about 1½ pounds)**
**2 tablespoons olive oil *or* salad oil**
**½ cup chopped onion**
**¼ cup chopped green pepper**
**⅓ cup dry white wine**
**1 16-ounce can tomatoes**
**2 8-ounce cans tomato sauce**
**1 6-ounce can tomato paste**
**1 clove garlic, minced**
**1 tablespoon snipped parsley**
**1 teaspoon dried oregano leaves, crushed**
**8 ounces spaghetti**
**1 6-ounce package sliced mozzarella cheese**

Brown the veal cutlets in oil. Remove meat. Add onion and green pepper; cook till tender. Stir in the next 7 ingredients. Add meat. Cover; simmer 30 minutes, stirring occasionally. Cook spaghetti according to package directions; drain. Remove *half* the sauce from meat; stir into spaghetti. Top the cutlets with cheese; cover the pan for 5 minutes. Arrange spaghetti and meat on platter; pass extra sauce and Parmesan cheese, if desired. Makes 6 servings.

## Spaghetti Turnover

**1 tablespoon salt**
**7 ounces spaghetti**
**½ cup chopped celery**
**¼ cup chopped onion**
**1 tablespoon poppy seed**
**½ teaspoon salt**
**¼ teaspoon pepper**
**½ cup light cream**
**8 ounces sharp natural Cheddar cheese, shredded (2 cups)**

Add 1 tablespoon salt to 3 quarts rapidly boiling water. Gradually add spaghetti so that water continues to boil. Cook, uncovered, stirring occasionally until just tender. Drain. Combine spaghetti, celery, onion, poppy seed, ½ teaspoon salt, pepper, and cream.

Lightly grease a large skillet; heat. Spoon *half* the spaghetti mixture into the skillet; top with 1½ *cups* of the Cheddar cheese. Top with remaining spaghetti mixture and sprinkle with remaining cheese. Cover and cook over medium heat, 25 to 30 minutes, running spatula under mixture occasionally to prevent sticking. Unmold onto serving platter. Garnish with parsley, if desired. Makes 6 servings.

## Beef and Spaghetti

**1 pound round steak, cut in cubes**
**2 tablespoons all-purpose flour**
**2 tablespoons shortening**
**½ cup chopped onion**
**1 clove garlic, minced**
**1 3-ounce can broiled, chopped mushrooms**
**1 10¾-ounce can condensed tomato soup**
**1 tablespoon Worcestershire sauce**
**3 drops bottled hot pepper sauce**
**1 cup dairy sour cream**
**Hot cooked spaghetti**

Coat meat with flour; brown in hot shortening. Add onion; cook till tender. Add garlic, undrained mushrooms, next 3 ingredients, ½ teaspoon salt, and dash pepper; mix. Cover and simmer till tender, about 1¼ hours; stir occasionally. Stir in sour cream and ¼ cup water; heat, *but do not boil.* Spoon over spaghetti. Pass Parmesan cheese, if desired. Serves 6.

**SPANISH COOKERY**—The traditional dishes of Spain, which are a blend of the country's history and its natural food resources. Since long before the Christian era, people have invaded, colonized, and captured this land. The new owners influenced the growth of the country. This included planting olive trees and grape vines in the fertile soil, and introducing many new foods from neighboring lands. In turn, when Spain sent her explorers and conquerors, the conquistadores, to the New World, they brought back many strange, new foods. Among them were tomatoes, potatoes, vanilla, and chocolate, all long since blended into the Spanish cuisine.

The fertile land of Spain grows good crops. From the wide variety of foods that grow abundantly, and the fish and shellfish from the seas that surround the peninsula, a recognizable Spanish cuisine developed. As in many countries, there are regional variations in the preparation of national dishes from province to province, partly due to the use of local seasonal foods, and partly due to the ingenuity and taste of those who cook.

***Characteristics of Spanish foods:*** Contrary to popular belief, Spanish food is not pungently hot. Too often it is confused with the Spanish-American cooking that makes generous use of the hot chili peppers. Yet these are practically unkown in Spain. However, garlic, olives, garbanzos (chickpeas), onion, saffron, and olive oil are ingredients that find their way into many of the Spanish dishes.

Fish and shellfish, especially along the coasts of Spain or near the rivers and streams that supply trout and salmon, are interestingly handled by Spanish cooks. Hearty fish soups are included among the seafood dishes prepared there.

Excellent young veal, lamb, pork, and chicken are Spain's principal meats, although good beef is also available. Wild game, such as wild boar and deer, and game birds, including quail, partridge, and pheasant, are also items frequently found in the Spanish cuisine.

Other foods that are served in Spain include fresh vegetables, many of which are used in cooked food mixtures. A simple green salad dressed with olive oil, vinegar, and seasonings is another favorite. Rice is grown mainly in the Valencia region of Spain and is used in a variety of dishes with chicken, seafood, or vegetables.

Both dry and sweet sherries are among the popular wines of Spain. Grapes for these wines are grown around Jerez in the southern-most province of Spain, which is considered the home of sherry. Sherry wines are used in preparing a great many dishes and sauces as well as being drunk as a food accompaniment.

The Spanish pattern of meals is simple, but meal hours are a bit startling to many visitors from other countries. Breakfast is a simple meal, usually quite early. The midday meal, around 2 p.m., is the hearty meal of the day, and dinner, really more like supper, is any time after 10 p.m. The long gaps between meals are filled with snacks or tiny meals of sweets or other types of foods. This is when *tapas,* appetizer-like foods, save the day. Many of these are made of seafood, vegetables, and cheese in bite-sized pieces that are just right for nibbling whenever hunger pangs strike any time of the day.

***Well-known recipes:*** Two Spanish soups are unique. One is *sopa de ajo,* a hot garlic soup that is essentially garlic, olive oil, bread, and water, with an egg added at the end. The other distinctive, classic soup is *gazpacho,* a unique salad-soup that is made differently in various provinces. Basic ingredients include tomato, cucumber, garlic, bread, olive oil, and vinegar. The result is a cold, refreshing soup. (See *Gazpacho* for recipe.)

*Paella,* the Spanish version of pilaf, is another classic dish that was born in Valencia. It is a mixture of chicken, shellfish, meat, vegetables, and rice. This dish, too, varies from region to region, with more or less saffron used in the rice, meat omitted entirely, and the seafood used according to the plentiful supply of seafood on hand. (See *Paella* for recipe.)

Countless dozen of eggs, *huevos,* are cooked according to many traditional and regional ways. If, however, you should see Spanish Omelet on a menu in Spain, don't expect it to be a big, puffy omelet served with a spicy tomato sauce as in America. It is likely to be a thick, hearty omelet with vegetables, such as potatoes and onion, or tomatoes, or seafood that are added to the beaten egg mixture.

Sweets usually accompany coffee or chocolate, sometimes at breakfast, but mostly as a late afternoon snack. *Churros*, made of doughnutlike dough pushed through a pastry tube into deep, hot fat to form circles, or sweet rich rolls are frequently served at breakfast.

Fresh fruits that grow abundantly in Spain are served as desserts, often accompanied by flavored sauces. Included in the wide variety of freshly grown fruits are grapes, oranges, lemons, figs, dates, strawberries, and melons. Other classic desserts include the caramel custard called *flan* (see *Flan* for recipe), and rice pudding with a cinnamon topping.

### Spanish Potato Omelet

**2 large potatoes, peeled and finely chopped (3 cups)**
**½ cup finely chopped onion**
**5 tablespoons olive oil**
**6 beaten eggs**
**⅓ cup milk**

In a 10-inch skillet cook potatoes and onion in *3 tablespoons* of the olive oil till tender, turning vegetables occasionally. Season with ½ teaspoon salt. Remove from heat.

Combine eggs, milk, ½ teaspoon salt, and dash pepper. Stir in cooked potato mixture. Heat remaining 2 tablespoons olive oil in same skillet. Pour in egg mixture. Cover and cook over low heat till omelet is nearly set, about 10 minutes. Invert omelet by placing plate over skillet and turning all over. Slide the omelet back into the skillet, moist side down. Cook omelet till underside is set, about 1 to 2 minutes. Loosen omelet and slide onto serving plate. Makes 4 servings.

**SPANISH CREAM**—A delicate molded dessert that is prepared with a soft custard of eggs, milk, and sugar, with gelatin added. The stiffly beaten egg whites are folded into the custard mixture, and as the dessert sets up when chilled in the refrigerator, it separates into two distinct layers, a foamy and a creamy mixture.

**SPANISH MACKEREL**—A saltwater fat fish that belongs to the mackerel family. The color of this fish is deep blue on the back and silvery below. Along the sides are three rows of gold-colored spots.

The Spanish mackerel is a popular fish along the east coast of the United States and is gaining adherents in other parts of the country. It can be found in the middle Atlantic during the summer months and off the Florida coast during the winter.

Because the scales of this fish are so very thin and fine, it does not have to be skinned or scaled before cooking. Preparation methods for this fat fish include broiling and baking. The fat on the fish keeps it moist during the period of cooking. Oftentimes, it is prepared with a tomato sauce. (See also *Mackerel*.)

**SPANISH SAUCE**—One of the classic brown sauces that is commonly called Espagnole. (See also *Espagnole Sauce*.)

**SPARERIB**—A cut of pork from the rib cage of a pig, containing the breastbone, rib bones, and rib cartilage, with a thin covering of meat. Spareribs are not to be confused with back ribs, also referred to as country-style back ribs, which are meatier or less "spare" ribs from the rib area of the loin section. The meat covering the back ribs comes from the loin eye.

Spareribs are available fresh and cured and smoked and should be cooked to the well-done stage by either roasting, braising, or cooking in liquid. Barbecued spareribs are also a popular method of preparation and are delicious cooked over charcoal and basted with a peppery sauce.

Like other cuts of pork, spareribs contribute protein to the diet and are a source of the B vitamins, especially thiamine. The meat from six plain, roasted medium ribs adds 246 calories to the diet. Sauces add a few additional calories, depending on their ingredients. Since there is generally a small amount of meat on spareribs, plan on about 1 to 1½ servings per pound of spareribs. (See also *Pork*.)

## Mustard Barbecued Ribs

**1 cup catsup**
**½ cup water**
**⅓ cup red wine vinegar**
**¼ cup salad oil**
**2 tablespoons instant minced onion**
**1 tablespoon brown sugar**
**1 tablespoon Worcestershire sauce**
**1 tablespoon whole mustard seed**
**2 teaspoons paprika**
**1 teaspoon dried oregano leaves, crushed**
**1 teaspoon chili powder**
**½ teaspoon salt**
**¼ teaspoon ground cloves**
**1 bay leaf**
**1 clove garlic, minced**
**4 pounds pork spareribs**

In small saucepan combine all ingredients except spareribs. Simmer, uncovered, 15 to 20 minutes, stirring once or twice. Remove bay leaf. Set sauce aside.

Sprinkle ribs with a little salt. Place ribs, meaty side down, in shallow roasting pan. Roast at 450° for 30 minutes. Remove meat from oven; drain off excess fat. Turn ribs, meaty side up. Reduce oven to 350°. Return ribs to oven; roast 1 hour more. Drain excess fat. Brush sauce over ribs; roast 30 minutes, basting occasionally with sauce. Serves 4 to 6.

## Spareribs Cantonese

**4 pounds pork spareribs, cut in serving-sized pieces**
**½ cup soy sauce**
**1 cup orange marmalade**
**½ teaspoon garlic powder**
**½ teaspoon ground ginger**

In a shallow roasting pan place ribs meaty side down. Roast at 450° for 30 minutes. Remove meat from oven; drain off excess fat. Turn ribs meaty side up. Reduce oven temperature to 350°; continue roasting ribs for 1 hour. In a small bowl combine soy sauce, ¾ cup water, orange marmalade, garlic powder, ginger, and dash pepper; blend thoroughly. Pour mixture over the ribs; roast till tender, about 30 minutes longer, basting ribs occasionally with the sauce. Makes 4 to 6 servings.

## Mincemeat Spareribs

**4 pounds pork spareribs, cut in serving-sized pieces**
**1 cup water**
**Salt**

. . .

**1½ cups prepared mincemeat**
**1 10½-ounce can condensed beef broth**
**2 tablespoons vinegar**

Place spareribs, meaty side up, in shallow roasting pan. Add water; sprinkle meat with a little salt. Cover pan with foil. Bake at 350° for 1½ hours; drain. Combine mincemeat, beef broth, and vinegar; pour over ribs in pan. Bake, uncovered, 30 to 45 minutes more, basting occasionally with pan juices. Serves 4 to 6.

## Luau Ribs

**2 4½-ounce jars or cans strained peaches (baby food)**
**⅓ cup catsup**
**⅓ cup vinegar**
**2 tablespoons soy sauce**
**½ cup brown sugar**
**1 clove garlic, minced**
**2 teaspoons ground ginger**
**1 teaspoon salt**
**Dash pepper**
**4 pounds meaty pork spareribs**

Mix together the strained peaches, catsup, vinegar, soy sauce, brown sugar, garlic, ginger, 1 teaspoon salt, and dash pepper. Rub the ribs with salt and pepper. Place the ribs, meaty side up, on a grill. Broil the ribs over *low* coals for about 20 minutes; turn meaty side down and broil till browned, about 10 minutes.

Again turn meaty side up, brush with peach sauce, and broil without turning till meat is well-done, about 30 minutes. Brush frequently with sauce. Makes 4 to 6 servings.

### *An unusual glaze for spareribs*

The topping for Mincemeat Spareribs is → concocted from prepared mincemeat, beef broth, and a hint of vinegar for tartness.

**SPARKLING WINE**—A wine that is made effervescent by natural means. Traditionally, as in champagne, the carbonation is trapped in the wine bottles when the wine is allowed to ferment a second time. In the newer Charmat process, secondary fermentation occurs in large, sealed tanks. To retain carbonation, the wine is then bottled under pressure. Some of the more popular sparkling wines include champagne, sparkling burgundy, and sparkling rosé. (See also *Wines and Spirits*.)

**SPATULA**—A utensil with a thin, flexible blade attached to a handle. The blade has no cutting edge. Available in a variety of styles, spatulas are used for spreading, turning, and lifting food.

**SPEARMINT**—A variety of the herbaceous mint plant used for flavoring food. Spearmint has been used for many centuries and was probably named after the spear- or lance-shaped arrangement of the flowers on the stem. The plant leaves are used to flavor candy, desserts, sauces, jellies, teas, and other beverages. (See also *Mint*.)

**SPECULAAS**—A spiced cookie that is traditionally served by the Dutch at Christmas. Carved wooden molds are sometimes used for shaping each cookie before baking.

### Speculaas

Thoroughly cream ½ cup butter or margarine and 1 cup brown sugar. Add 1 egg and 2 tablespoons milk; beat well. Sift together 2½ cups sifted all-purpose flour, 2 teaspoons baking powder, ½ teaspoon salt, 1 teaspoon ground cinnamon, ½ teaspoon ground cloves, and ½ teaspoon ground nutmeg. Blend into mixture.

Divide dough into thirds; chill.* Roll each portion on floured surface to 9x8-inch rectangle. Cut in twelve 3x2-inch pieces. Place on lightly greased cookie sheet. Sprinkle with ½ cup sliced almonds. Bake at 375° till lightly browned, 10 to 12 minutes. Makes 3 dozen.

*For molded cookies: Press chilled dough into well-floured mold. (Use only one mold at a time.) Remove immediately by turning mold over and tapping on the back. Use a knife point to remove cookie from mold, if necessary.

**SPELT**—A variety of wheat of economic importance in Europe, but only grown in small quantities in the United States.

**SPICE**—Any aromatic or fragrant part of a plant used to flavor and season food. Spices may include the berry, root, bark, kernel, fruit, or flower bud from the plant. Although the broad classification of spices encompasses the aromatic plants known as herbs, the following distinction is often used: spices come from tropical plants, while herbs grow in temperate regions.

The history of spices is ancient and filled with endless lore. Prized highly for their medicinal, aromatic, and savory properties, spices triggered explorations to unknown lands and helped shape the economic development of many countries.

Archaeologists believe that primitive man discovered the art of seasoning by accident, probably when he wrapped meat in leaves to keep it relatively free from ashes while it was being cooked over an open fire. It's not too difficult to imagine his astonishment when he unwrapped the meat and tasted the seasoned food.

According to the chiseled stone tablets of the ancient Assyrians, spices were used thousands of years before Christ. The Assyrians claimed that the gods drank sesame seed wine before creating the earth. Other references to spices are found in the *Holy Bible* as well as on pyramid walls.

In ancient times, trade routes were established on land and sea for the purpose of bringing spices back from the Orient to the Western world. Caravans brought pepper and cloves from India, ginger from China, and cinnamon and nutmeg from the Spice Islands. A safe return was not assured, as pirates, robbers, shipwrecks, and storms often were encountered.

Due to the limited supply, spices commanded a high price in the market place, and only the wealthy could afford them. Nevertheless, the uses for spices quickly multiplied. Crowns of bay leaves were awarded to Olympic heroes; spice-scented baths were a luxury enjoyed by the rich; temples were filled with the aroma of incense made from spices; medicinal remedies were prepared from spices; and spice-flavored wines and foods were delicacies.

In the Middle Ages, spices were frequently used as payment for taxes and rent. Pepper was the most valuable of all the spices. Each peppercorn was counted individually, whereas other spices generally were traded in weight measure. For example, one pound of ginger was a fair exchange for one sheep, while one pound of mace was equivalent to three sheep or half a cow. Because of the preciousness of spices, dock guards in London were required to stitch their pockets shut to guard against thievery as spices were unloaded from incoming ships. Despite the risks involved, the spice trade flourished.

As early as 950 B.C., the Arabs controlled the spice routes. They kept other potential spice traders from entering the market by relating tales of piracy and danger which they faced along the spice routes. The Arabs were successful in keeping the source of the spices a secret from European traders for some time.

The travels of Marco Polo, which began around 1271, revealed the source of many spices, and European merchants quickly realized they could secure the valuable spices by sea. Competition for control of the routes increased as England, Spain, Portugal, and Holland raced to the Orient to bring back the valuable merchandise.

The quest for spices resulted in the discovery of new lands. Columbus's famous voyage in search of a new route to the Orient, led him to the discovery of America, and other countries also sent out expeditions to find new trade routes. Although many of the ventures ended unsuccessfully, the search for spices continued.

During the 1500s, the English concentrated on finding trade routes to the North, since the Spaniards held the routes to the west and the Portuguese controlled the eastward routes. Although the English were unsuccessful in reaching the spice countries by traveling north, they made important and strategic navigational discoveries. In doing so, they established themselves as a mighty sea power by the end of the sixteenth century.

The following century, the Dutch gained control of the Portuguese-held spice ports in the Indies and established the Dutch East Indies. The Dutch stranglehold was so powerful that they often burned or destroyed excess spices to keep the prices high. They continued their monopoly of the spice trade for almost 200 years. However, by 1799, English sea victories resulted in the liquidation of the monopoly.

Whole cloves and bay leaf season Spicy Chops and Cabbage. To complete this skillet meal, add diced apple for color and flavor.

The British were helped greatly by the French, for while the French government did little to promote the search for spices, French sea captains discovered southern routes and the spice-rich islands of the Atlantic. Although the French were unable to establish a monopoly along the southern routes, their efforts did aid the fall of the Dutch spice monopoly.

At about the same time, American sea captains entered the market by sailing from Salem, Massachusetts, to Sumatra and back. For about 100 years, American vessels returned loaded with black pepper.

Today, the spice trade is still a very prosperous business, although the means of securing these aromatic plants is no longer the mission of danger and mystery it was centuries ago. Most spices are now readily available at a reasonable cost.

Almost every country in the world produces some spice; however, the tropical spices are still obtained in greatest quantity from the original spice-rich countries in the East. Some of the spices supplied by countries in the Americas include ginger and allspice from Jamaica, nutmeg from Grenada, sesame seed from Nicaragua and Salvador, and fenugreek seed from Argentina. Spices produced in the United States are sesame seed, laurel, basil, tarragon, mustard, chili powder, paprika, and red pepper. Since the supply of American-grown spices is small, it is necessary to import a major portion of all spices used in the United States.

***Classification of spices:*** There are various methods for classifying spices. If grouped according to properties, spices are divided into three categories—stimulating condiments (black pepper, capsicum peppers, garlic, horseradish, and mustard); aromatic spices (anise, cardamon, cinnamon, cloves, and ginger); and sweet herbs (basil, chervil, fennel, parsley, and sage).

Spices are often arranged according to the plant families to which they belong. Some of the larger families include the *Libiatae*, or mint family; the *Umbelliferae*, or parsley family; the *Compositae*, or aster family; and the *Liliaceae*, or lily family.

It is also possible to classify the great number of spices according to the plant part from which they are refined. For example, the plant parts and their respective spices include the dried flower bud (cloves); the fruit (allspice, black pepper, nutmeg, and vanilla); the underground root (ginger, horseradish, and turmeric); the bark (cinnamon); and the seed or seed-like structures (anise, caraway, cardamom, coriander, dill, poppy, and sesame).

***Forms of spices:*** Most spices are imported in whole form and are checked by government inspectors before they go to a grinding company. Some of the more popular spices marketed in whole form include allspice, cinnamon, cloves, ginger, black pepper, red pepper, and saffron.

Many spices are also sold in ground form. Those available in most supermarkets include allspice, cardamom, celery seed, cinnamon, cloves, coriander, cumin, ginger, mace, mustard, nutmeg, paprika, black pepper, red pepper, white pepper, saffron, turmeric, and some sweet herbs. Since food manufacturers often prefer a finer or coarser grind than that used in the home, spice processors offer many grinds.

Spice blends are prepared from a mixture of herbs and spices and are sometimes preferred by the homemaker for cooking purposes. Popular spice blends include apple pie spice, cinnamon sugar, barbecue spice, chili powder, curry powder, herb seasoning, Italian seasoning, mixed pickling spice, poultry seasoning, pumpkin pie spice, seafood seasoning, seasoned or flavored salt, and shrimp spice.

***How to store:*** Spices maintain their flavor longer when stored in a cool, dry place. Avoid keeping spices in warm areas of the kitchen. Also, store spices in a tightly covered container. Exposure to air increases flavor loss. Generally, whole spices have a longer storage life than ground spices. In areas subject to prolonged hot temperatures, spices such as paprika, crushed red pepper, cayenne, chili powder, and aromatic seeds are best stored in the refrigerator.

To determine the freshness of a spice, note the color and flavor. When fresh, most spices have a bright, rich color and a readily apparent aroma when the container is opened. If either color or aroma appears weak, replace the spice.

***How to use:*** Whole spices are ideal for seasoning hot beverages, soups, stews, and other foods that have long, slow cooking, as the flavor of the spice is released slowly with moist heat. To use, place whole spices in a cheesecloth bag for easy removal. If whole spices are added to an uncooked marinade, let the marinade stand several hours, as more time is needed to extract the flavor in a cold mixture.

Ground spices, which provide a more instant flavor, are excellent used in baked products, salads, desserts, casseroles, and other short-cooking or unbaked foods. Since the flavor of the ground spice is released quickly, add the spice near the end of the cooking period unless the cooking time is short. Ground spices, such as cinnamon or nutmeg, also are attractive when they are sprinkled over a dessert or salad as a garnish. (See also *Herb*.)

*Seasoning guide for spices*

**Allspice**
- Baked ham
- Beef stew
- Cake
- Cookies
- Meat loaf
- Pot roast
- Pumpkin pie
- Shellfish
- Tomato sauce
- Vegetable soup

**Cinnamon**
- Apples
- Cake
- Cookies
- Hot cereal
- Prune butter
- Pudding
- Spiced fruit

**Cloves**
- Chocolate pudding
- Fruitcake
- Fruit pastries
- Ham
- Roast pork
- Spiced fruit
- Stew

**Ginger**
- Carrots
- Chicken
- Cookies
- Fruit pastries
- Marmalade
- Pears
- Pot roast
- Pudding
- Spice cake
- Stew
- Sweet potatoes

**Mace**
- Cherry pie
- Chocolate desserts
- Creamed eggs
- Cream sauce
- Fish sauce
- Fruit cobbler
- Meat stuffing
- Oyster stew
- Pound cake
- Welsh rabbit

**Nutmeg**
- Bananas
- Beef
- Chicken Soup
- Creamed vegetables
- Custard
- Doughnuts
- Eggnog
- Fish
- Pears
- Rice pudding

**Paprika**
- Chicken
- Chili
- Cream sauce
- Eggs
- Fish
- Potatoes
- Veal

**Pepper—Black**
- Barbecue sauce
- Gravy
- Stew
- Vegetable soup

**Pepper—Red**
- Cheese dishes
- Chowder
- Cream soup
- Deviled ham
- Eggs
- Pasta
- Seafood
- Stew

**Pepper—White**
- Chicken
- Cream soup
- Fish
- Ham
- Mayonnaise
- Poultry

**Saffron**
- Bread
- Cake
- Rice
- Tea

**Turmeric**
- Creamed eggs
- Fish
- Pickles
- Relishes

## Spicy Chops and Cabbage

**4 pork loin chops**
**2 tablespoons water**
**½ teaspoon salt**
**2 whole cloves**
**½ small bay leaf**
**1 medium head cabbage, coarsely shredded (8 cups)**
**1½ cups diced, tart apple**
**¼ cup chopped onion**
**¼ cup sugar**
**1½ teaspoons all-purpose flour**
**½ teaspoon salt**
**2 tablespoons vinegar**
**2 tablespoons water**

Trim fat from chops. In skillet cook trimmings till small amount of fat accumulates; discard trimmings. Brown chops in accumulated fat. Add 2 tablespoons water, salt, cloves, and bay leaf; cover and simmer for 30 minutes.

Remove chops from skillet; discard cloves and bay leaf. Add cabbage, apple, and onion. Combine sugar, flour, and ½ teaspoon salt. Stir in vinegar and 2 tablespoons water. Pour over cabbage, stirring to mix. Cover and simmer for 5 minutes. Return pork chops to skillet; cover and cook till chops and cabbage are tender, 20 minutes longer. Makes 4 servings.

## Gingered Ham Slice

**1 fully cooked center cut ham slice, 1 inch thick**

. . .

**½ cup ginger ale**
**½ cup orange juice**
**¼ cup brown sugar**
**1 tablespoon salad oil**
**1½ teaspoons wine vinegar**
**1 teaspoon dry mustard**
**¼ teaspoon ground ginger**
**⅛ teaspoon ground cloves**

Slash fat edge of ham. Combine ginger ale and remaining ingredients; in shallow dish pour mixture over ham. Refrigerate overnight or let stand at room temperature 2 hours, spooning marinade over ham several times. Broil ham slice over *low* coals about 15 minutes on each side; brush often with marinade. To serve, spoon marinade over ham. Serves 5 or 6.

Polynesian Pork Steaks, reminiscent of other island specialties, simmer slowly in a tangy sauce made with ginger and coconut.

## Polynesian Pork Steaks

**6 pork arm or blade steaks**
**2 tablespoons salad oil**
**1 4¾-ounce jar strained plums (baby food)**
**¼ cup flaked coconut**
**1 tablespoon vinegar**
**1 tablespoon salad oil**
**2 teaspoons soy sauce**
**½ teaspoon ground ginger**
**½ teaspoon grated lemon peel**

In skillet brown steaks in salad oil. Sprinkle with salt. Combine remaining ingredients, 2 tablespoons water, ½ teaspoon salt, and dash pepper; pour around steaks. Cover; simmer till tender, 35 to 40 minutes. Remove steaks to platter; spoon sauce over. Serves 6.

## Spicy Fruit Dressing

In mixing bowl combine 1 cup dairy sour cream, ½ cup apple cider *or* apple juice, ½ cup salad oil, ½ teaspoon ground cinnamon, ¼ teaspoon ground nutmeg, and dash salt; beat with rotary beater till smooth. Chill thoroughly. Serve with fruit salads. Makes 2 cups.

## Cran-Cheese Squares

**1 3-ounce package orange-pineapple-flavored gelatin**
**1 cup orange juice**
**½ cup whipping cream**
**1 3-ounce package cream cheese, softened**
**¼ cup chopped pecans**
**. . .**
**1 envelope unflavored gelatin (1 tablespoon)**
**1 16-ounce can whole cranberry sauce**
**2 tablespoons lemon juice**
**¼ teaspoon ground allspice**
**⅛ teaspoon ground nutmeg**
**1 cup orange sections**
**1 7-ounce bottle ginger ale, chilled (about 1 cup)**

Dissolve orange-pineapple-flavored gelatin in 1 cup boiling water; stir in orange juice. Chill till partially set. Whip cream. Blend a little whipped cream into cream cheese; fold in remaining whipped cream. Add nuts; fold cream mixture into gelatin. Pour into 9x9x2-inch pan; chill till *almost* firm.

Soften unflavored gelatin in ¼ cup cold water; stir over low heat till dissolved. Combine cranberry sauce, lemon juice, allspice, nutmeg, and orange sections; stir in gelatin. Slowly pour ginger ale down side of bowl; stir gently to mix. Pour slowly over cheese layer. Chill till firm. To serve, cut into squares. Makes 9 servings.

## Spiced Peaches

**5 cups sugar**
**2 cups water**
**1 cup vinegar**
**12 inches stick cinnamon, broken**
**2 teaspoons whole cloves**
**Small peaches, peeled**

Combine sugar, water, vinegar, cinnamon, and cloves; heat to boiling. Into syrup drop enough peaches to fill 2 or 3 pints. Heat mixture about 5 minutes. Pack fruit in hot pint jars; add syrup to within ½ inch of top. Adjust lids. Process in boiling water bath for 20 minutes (count time after water returns to boil). Seven pounds fresh peaches yields 9 pints fruit.

## Spicy Coconut Chiffon Pie

**1 cup flaked coconut**
**1 teaspoon ground cinnamon**
**1/4 teaspoon ground ginger**
**1/8 teaspoon ground mace**
**1 envelope unflavored gelatin**
**1/2 cup sugar**
**1 1/4 cups milk**
**4 beaten egg yolks**
**1 teaspoon vanilla**
**1/4 teaspoon cream of tartar**
**4 egg whites**
**1/2 cup whipping cream**
**1 baked 9-inch pastry shell cooled (See *Pastry*)**

Mix first 4 ingredients; spread in shallow pan. Toast at 350° till coconut is brown, about 8 minutes; stir occasionally. In saucepan combine gelatin, sugar, and 1/4 teaspoon salt. Slowly stir in milk. Add egg yolks. Cook and stir over low heat till mixture thickens. Stir in vanilla. Cool thoroughly.

In large mixer bowl add cream of tartar to egg whites; beat till stiff but not dry. Whip cream. Fold egg whites and whipped cream into yolk mixture. Chill till partially set. Pile *half* of the chiffon mixture in pastry shell. Sprinkle *half* of the coconut over filling. Repeat layers; chill. To serve, garnish with additional whipped cream, if desired.

## Spice-Nut Cake

Sift together 2 cups sifted all-purpose flour, 1 cup granulated sugar, 1 teaspoon baking powder, 1 teaspoon salt, 3/4 teaspoon *each* baking soda, ground cloves, and ground cinnamon. Add 2/3 cup shortening, 3/4 cup brown sugar, and 1 cup buttermilk *or* sour milk.

Mix till all flour is moistened. Beat 2 minutes at medium speed on electric mixer. Add 3 eggs; beat 2 minutes more. Stir in 1/2 cup finely chopped walnuts. Pour into 2 greased and lightly floured 9x1 1/2-inch round pans. Bake at 350° till done, 30 to 35 minutes. Cool 10 minutes; remove from pans. Cool completely.

Frost with *Maple Fluff Frosting:* In 1-quart saucepan boil 1 cup maple-flavored syrup over medium heat for 5 minutes. Gradually pour hot syrup over 3 stiffly beaten egg whites, beating constantly till frosting forms soft peaks.

## Spicy Prune Cake

**1 1/2 cups sifted all-purpose flour**
**3/4 cup granulated sugar**
**1/4 cup brown sugar**
**1 teaspoon baking powder**
**1/2 teaspoon baking soda**
**1/2 teaspoon ground cinnamon**
**1/4 teaspoon salt**
**1/4 teaspoon ground ginger**
**1/2 cup cold water**
**1/2 cup salad oil**
**1 4 3/4-ounce jar strained prunes (baby food)**
**1 egg**
**1 teaspoon vanilla**
**1/2 cup chopped walnuts**

• • •

**1/2 cup sifted confectioners' sugar**
**1/8 teaspoon ground cinnamon**
**1 tablespoon light cream**

In mixer bowl sift together flour, granulated sugar, brown sugar, baking powder, baking soda, 1/2 teaspoon cinnamon, salt, and ginger. Add water and next 4 ingredients. Blend; beat 1 minute at medium speed of electric mixer.

Turn into greased and floured 9x9x2-inch baking pan. Sprinkle nuts over batter. Bake at 350° for 30 minutes; cool cake in pan. Mix remaining ingredients. Drizzle over cake.

Sprinkle chopped nuts over Spicy Prune Cake batter before baking. When cool, drizzle nut-topped cake with confectioners' icing.

**SPIDER**—An old-time name for a heavy, three-legged iron pot or pan that was set over fireplace coals for cooking.

**SPINACH**—An annual, dark green, leafy vegetable that is eaten raw or cooked.

Although most spinach culinary history has been lost, its origin has been pinpointed to southwestern Asia. Spinach plants existed in this area many centuries ago, but how cultivation and use spread is unclear. Some historians believe that spinach was used by the Chinese prior to its introduction to Greece, Italy, and Spain, while others disagree.

***How spinach is produced:*** Spinach plants have a short-term growth cycle that necessitates specific climate and soil conditions for optimum leaf development. As the plants take only eight weeks to mature, the seeds often are sown between the rows of slower-growing crops. The plants require cool weather and rich, sandy, well-watered, well-limed soil. Spinach is planted in the South during the winter and in other regions in the spring and fall.

***Nutritional value:*** One serving of cooked spinach (½ cup) provides only 21 calories. This portion also adds outstanding amounts of vitamins and minerals to the diet. It is an excellent source of vitamin A, iron, and B vitamin riboflavin, and, if raw or properly cooked, vitamin C. Niacin is present in moderate amounts.

***Types of spinach:*** There are fewer spinach varieties used for commercial production than for some other vegetables. The two most important types are the Broad Flanders and the New Zealand spinach.

***How to select and store:*** Choose spinach leaves that are large and fresh-looking, and have good green color. Avoid leaves with wilted or yellow areas. Since fresh spinach shrinks when it is cooked, count on one pound of the fresh leaves yielding about 1½ cups cooked. Frozen or canned spinach is available also.

Even the freshest spinach maintains its quality for only a few days, so, for best storage results, wrap or cover the leaves, and place them in the vegetable crisper. Add crushed ice to the spinach package to help hold the leaves at peak quality.

***How to prepare:*** Spinach lovers attest to the fact that proper washing and cooking are essential to remove sand. Because spinach grows low to the ground, the leaves often contain small amounts of sand. To remove it, place a bunch of leaves in a pan of lukewarm water. After a few minutes, lift them out. Drain the leaves and discard the now-sandy water. Repeat several times more until no sand appears in the bottom of the pan. This warm water method more easily removes the sand than would washing each leaf under cold water.

The flavor of spinach is best retained when the leaves are cooked only in the water that clings to the washed leaves. Reduce the heat when the steam begins to form, and cook spinach, covered, for three to five minutes. Turn leaves often with a fork. For optimum nutritional value, use a small amount of water while cooking.

***How to serve:*** Whether fresh, frozen, or canned, whole leaves or chopped, spinach is an attractive vegetable when properly cooked. In salads, uncooked fresh spinach is used for color and flavor or as a substitute for lettuce.

Spinach combines well with a host of seasonings and foods. Allspice, basil, cinnamon, dill, marjoram, mint, nutmeg, oregano, rosemary, or sesame seed is used with spinach in the cooking liquid, or for salads, in the salad dressing. Hard-cooked egg, chopped or sliced, is a popular addition to raw or cooked spinach. Creamy sauces are used as toppings or in casseroles. Among these, any dish with Florentine in the title is sure to contain spinach. (See also *Vegetable*.)

## Spinach-Avocado Bowl

Place 10 ounces fresh spinach, torn in bite-sized pieces, in salad bowl. Arrange 2 medium avocados, peeled and sliced; ½ pound bacon, crisp-cooked, drained, and crumbled; and ½ cup chopped peanuts over spinach. Serve with Russian-style salad dressing. Serves 8 to 10.

The flavor essence and fine texture of fresh spinach—Popeye's favorite vegetable—is preserved when served uncooked in salads or when cooked in the water that clings to the leaves.

## Orange-Spinach Toss

- **4 cups fresh spinach, torn in bite-sized pieces**
- **3 oranges, peeled and sectioned**
- **4 slices bacon, crisp-cooked, drained, and crumbled**
- **½ cup chopped peanuts**
- **1 envelope French-style salad dressing mix**

In a salad bowl combine spinach, orange sections, bacon, and peanuts. Prepare French-style salad dressing mix according to package directions. Pour desired amount over spinach mixture. Toss lightly to coat. Makes 4 servings.

## Spinach-Lettuce Toss

- **5 slices bacon**
- **3 cups torn leaf lettuce**
- **3 cups torn, fresh spinach**
- **¼ cup diced celery**
- **2 tablespoons crumbled blue cheese**
- **1 tablespoon chopped green onion**
- **¼ cup vinegar**
- **2 tablespoons sugar**
- **½ teaspoon Worcestershire sauce**

Cook bacon till crisp. Drain; reserving drippings. Crumble bacon; combine with next 5 ingredients. To drippings, add remaining ingredients; bring to a boil. Toss with salad. Serves 6.

## Wilted Spinach Salad

**1 pound fresh spinach**
**½ cup sliced green onion**
**Dash freshly ground pepper**
**. . .**
**5 slices bacon, diced**
**2 tablespoons wine vinegar**
**1 tablespoon lemon juice**
**1 teaspoon sugar**
**½ teaspoon salt**
**1 hard-cooked egg, coarsely chopped**

Wash the spinach, discarding the stems. Pat dry on paper toweling; tear in bite-sized pieces into a salad bowl. Add the sliced green onion. Sprinkle with pepper. Chill.

At serving time, slowly fry bacon in deep chafing dish or electric skillet till crisp-cooked. Add vinegar, lemon juice, sugar, and salt. Gradually add spinach, tossing just till the leaves are coated and wilted slightly. Sprinkle the salad with chopped egg. Serve immediately. Makes 4 to 6 servings.

## Tuna-Spinach Toss

**2 cups torn spinach**
**1 cup torn lettuce**
**½ small red onion, thinly sliced and separated into rings (about ½ cup)**
**1 6½- or 7-ounce can tuna, drained and flaked**
**4 ounces Swiss cheese, cut into narrow 2-inch strips (about 1 cup)**
**. . .**
**¼ cup olive *or* salad oil**
**1 tablespoon vinegar**
**1 tablespoon lemon juice**
**½ teaspoon salt**
**¼ teaspoon dried tarragon leaves, crushed**

Toss spinach and lettuce in large salad bowl. Place onion rings around sides of bowl. Heap tuna in center; surround with cheese. Combine olive oil, vinegar, lemon juice, salt, tarragon, and dash pepper in screw-top jar; shake well. Just before serving, toss dressing mixture with salad. Makes 4 servings.

## Tangy Spinach Toss

**2 tablespoons sliced green onion**
**¼ cup butter or margarine**
**2 tablespoons all-purpose flour**
**¼ teaspoon salt**
**1 cup water**
**2 tablespoons lemon juice**
**1 tablespoon prepared horseradish**
**½ teaspoon Worcestershire sauce**
**. . .**
**2 hard-cooked eggs**
**1 pound fresh spinach, torn in bite-sized pieces**
**Paprika**

Cook onion in butter about 1 minute; blend in flour and salt. Add water, lemon juice, horseradish, and Worcestershire sauce; cook and stir till mixture boils.

Dice *one* egg; add to dressing. Pour dressing over spinach in salad bowl; toss lightly. Slice remaining egg for garnish; sprinkle with paprika. Serve at once. Serves 6 to 8.

## Spinach Surprise

**1 pound fresh spinach**
**2 tablespoons butter or margarine**
**¼ cup light cream**
**½ tablespoon prepared horseradish**
**Hard-cooked egg slices**

Cook spinach; drain and chop. Add butter, cream, and horseradish. Heat through. Season to taste with salt and pepper. Garnish with hard-cooked egg slices. Makes 3 or 4 servings.

## Chinese Spinach

**1 pound fresh spinach**
**2 tablespoons salad oil**
**1 tablespoon soy sauce**

Wash and pat dry the spinach leaves. Remove stems and cut into 1-inch pieces; tear leaves into bite-sized pieces. Heat salad oil and soy sauce in skillet; add spinach. Cover and cook just till wilted, about 1 minute. Uncover; cook and toss till spinach is crisp-tender and well-coated, about 2 minutes. Makes 4 servings.

For Tangy Spinach Toss, a new version of salad dressing coats fresh spinach leaves. Minus oil or mayonnaise, the thickened mixture blends lemon juice, horseradish, and Worcestershire.

## Spinach Supreme

**2 10-ounce packages frozen chopped spinach**
**1½ cups milk**
**2 slightly beaten eggs**
**1 1¾-ounce envelope dry cream of leek soup mix**

Cook spinach according to package directions; drain thoroughly. Combine milk and eggs; gradually stir into the soup mix. Add spinach and mix well. Turn into a 10x6x1½-inch baking dish. Bake at 350° until the edges of the casserole are set, but center is still creamy, about 30 minutes. Serves 6 to 8.

## Spinach-Potato Bake

**1 10¼-ounce can frozen condensed cream of potato soup, thawed *or* 1 10½-ounce can condensed cream of potato soup**
**1 10-ounce package frozen chopped spinach, thawed**
**2 beaten eggs**
**1 teaspoon instant minced onion**
**Dash salt**

Combine all ingredients and dash pepper, mixing well. Turn into lightly greased 10x6x1½-inch baking dish. Bake, uncovered, at 350° for 30 minutes. Makes 4 to 6 servings.

## Spinach Elegante

- 2 10-ounce packages frozen chopped spinach
- 3 slices bacon, crisp-cooked, drained, and crumbled
- 1 6-ounce can sliced mushrooms, drained (1 cup)
- 1/4 teaspoon dried marjoram leaves, crushed
- 1 cup dairy sour cream
- 1/2 cup shredded sharp process American cheese

Cook spinach according to package directions. Drain well; spread on bottom of a 10x6x1½-inch baking dish. Arrange bacon and mushrooms over. Sprinkle with dash pepper and marjoram. Bake at 325° for 15 minutes. Cover with sour cream and cheese. Heat in oven till cheese melts, about 5 minutes. Serves 6.

## Spinach Delight

- 2 10-ounce packages frozen chopped spinach, cooked and drained
- 4 slices bacon, crisp-cooked drained, and crumbled
- 1 5-ounce can water chestnuts, drained and sliced
- 1 10-ounce package frozen Welsh rarebit, thawed (about 1 cup)
- 1 cup canned French-fried onions

Place the cooked spinach in a 10x6x1½-inch baking dish. Top with bacon and water chestnuts. Spread Welsh rarebit evenly over top. Garnish with the canned French-fried onions. Bake at 350° till heated through, about 20 to 25 minutes. Makes 6 to 8 servings.

## Épinards à la Crème (Creamed Spinach)

Chop and drain 1 pound fresh cooked spinach, Add ¼ cup medium white sauce (see *White Sauce*), ½ teaspoon salt, dash pepper, dash Worcestershire sauce, and dash bottled hot pepper sauce. Mix thoroughly. Spread into an 8-inch pie plate. Top with ¼ cup hollandaise sauce (see *Hollandaise Sauce*). Brown lightly at 425° for 15 minutes. Makes 4 servings.

## Shrimp à la Rockefeller

- 1/4 cup butter or margarine
- 1 teaspoon celery seed
- 1 teaspoon Worcestershire sauce
- 1 cup chopped lettuce
- 1/4 cup chopped green onion
- 1 small clove garlic, minced
- 2 10-ounce packages frozen chopped spinach, thawed and drained
- 1 cup light cream
- 1 beaten egg
- 8 ounces cleaned, cooked shrimp
- 2 tablespoons butter, melted
- 1/4 cup fine dry bread crumbs
- 1/4 cup grated Parmesan cheese

In medium saucepan combine ¼ cup butter, celery seed, Worcestershire sauce, and ½ teaspoon salt. Stir in lettuce, green onion, and garlic; simmer, covered, 2 to 3 minutes. Add the spinach, cream, and beaten egg. Cook and stir till mixture begins to simmer. Divide *half* the shrimp among four individual casseroles or 8-ounce baking shells. Add hot spinach mixture. Top with remaining shrimp. Combine 2 tablespoons melted butter, bread crumbs, and cheese. Sprinkle evenly over the casseroles. Bake at 375° just till hot, about 15 minutes. Makes 4 servings.

## Spinach-Carrot Custard

- 1/4 cup butter or margarine
- 1/4 cup all-purpose flour
- 1 1/2 cups milk
- 1 tablespoon instant minced onion
- 2 slightly beaten eggs
- 1 1/2 cups shredded carrots, cooked and drained
- 1 10-ounce package frozen chopped spinach, cooked and drained

In saucepan melt butter; blend in flour. Add milk, onion, and ½ teaspoon salt. Cook and stir till mixture thickens and bubbles. Remove from heat. Stir small amount of hot sauce into eggs. Return to hot mixture and cook till blended, stirring constantly. Add carrots and spinach. Pour into eight 5-ounce custard cups. Bake at 325° till knife inserted halfway between center and edge comes out clean, about 20 to 25 minutes. Makes 8 servings.

**SPINACH NOODLE**—A type of pasta, also known as a green noodle, that gets its characteristic color and flavor from the finely chopped spinach that is added to the basic dough. When making spinach noodles at home, use an electric blender to chop the spinach, if possible. Commercially made spinach noodles in one or more of the classic shapes are found in Italian food stores and some supermarkets.

**SPINY LOBSTER**—Another name for the crayfish or rock lobster. (See *Crayfish, Lobster* for additional information.)

**SPIRIT**—A highly alcoholic liquid that is made by distilling the fermented juice of foods such as grains, sugars, fruits, and vegetables. Brandy, gin, rum, vodka, whiskey, and liqueurs are among spirits used both as beverages and as recipe ingredients. (See also *Wines and Spirits.*)

**SPIT** – A large skewer or turning rod on which food is balanced for rotisserie cooking. (See also *Rotisserie.*)

**SPLIT**—**1.** To cut a food into two parts or to divide a food into its natural parts by applying pressure or a sharp point to a seam or natural line of division. **2.** An ice cream sundae that derives its name from the fruit cut in half lengthwise and arranged on the bottom of the dessert dish. **3.** The name given to the small beverage bottle that contains about six ounces.

Chickens are split lengthwise for broiling or grilling. English muffins are split with a fork before toasting, and peas that did not separate during drying are split mechanically to make split peas.

For dessert splits, several scoops of ice cream, either vanilla or assorted flavors, are placed in a row on top of the fruit. Sundae toppings are spooned over ice cream and fruit, and the dessert is capped with whipped cream, chopped nuts, and a cherry. Bananas are popular for splits because the long strips of fruit are attractive and the flavor is delicious with many flavors of ice cream and toppings.

The split bottle is mainly used for wine, especially champagne, and holds about one-quarter the amount of a regular bottle.

**SPLIT PEA**—Dry peas, either green or yellow, from which the thin skins have been removed, allowing the seeds to split apart at the natural breaking point. Some of the splitting takes place while the peas are drying; the balance, during processing.

Soaking split peas before cooking is necessary only if you wish to retain the shape in a finished dish such as when baking them like dry beans with pork. First, add split peas to boiling water; boil two minutes. Remove from heat; cover and let soak for a half hour. (See also *Pea.*)

## Split Pea Soup

**1 pound green or yellow split peas (2¼ cups)**
**2 quarts cold water**
**1 meaty ham bone (1½ pounds)**
**1½ cups sliced onion**
**1 teaspoon salt**
**½ teaspoon pepper**
**¼ teaspoon dried marjoram leaves, crushed**

. . .

**1 cup diced carrots**
**1 cup diced celery**

In a large saucepan cover split peas with the 2 quarts cold water. Add ham bone, sliced onion, salt, pepper, and marjoram. Bring mixture to boiling; cover, reduce heat, and simmer (*don't boil*) 1½ hours. Stir soup mixture occasionally. Remove ham bone from soup; cut off meat and dice. Return meat to soup; add diced carrots and celery. Cook slowly, uncovered, 30 to 40 minutes. Serves 6 to 8.

**SPONGE**—**1.** A light, frothy dessert that gains its lightness and porous texture from the air incorporated into it by folding in beaten egg whites or gelatin, which is whipped when partially set.

**2.** Yeast bread dough after the first stage of rising in the "sponge" method of breadmaking. A batter of yeast, liquid, and some of the flour, allowed to rise until bubbly, resembles a sponge. Then, the remaining ingredients are added and breadmaking proceeds as usual. (See *Bread, Dessert* for additional information.)

**SPONGE CAKE**—A moist, yellow cake containing egg yolks that is traditionally made without shortening and which gets most of its volume from the air trapped in the egg whites folded into the batter.

In years past, before home freezers made freezing egg yolks practical, homemakers baked the egg yolk version of sponge cake as a companion to an angel food cake that was made from the egg whites. Today, most sponge cake recipes call for whole eggs, but occasionally you will find a recipe that uses more egg yolks.

When mixing a sponge cake, beat the egg yolks and the egg whites separately. First, beat the yolks and a liquid, such as fruit juice like orange or pineapple juice, until thick and lemon-colored. Then add flour and part of the sugar to the yolk mixture. Next, beat together the whites, cream of tartar, if used, and the remaining sugar. Finally, gently fold the batter into the egg whites, retaining as much air as possible. The cake is customarily baked in an ungreased tube cake pan.

## Orange Sponge Cake

**1⅓ cups sifted cake flour**
**⅓ cup sugar**
**6 egg yolks**
**1 tablespoon grated orange peel**
**½ cup orange juice**
**⅔ cup sugar**
**¼ teaspoon salt**
**6 egg whites**
**1 teaspoon cream of tartar**
**½ cup sugar**

Combine sifted cake flour and the ⅓ cup sugar. Set aside. Beat egg yolks till thick and lemon-colored. Add the grated orange peel and orange juice; beat till very thick. Gradually add the ⅔ cup sugar and salt, beating constantly. Sift flour mixture over egg yolk mixture, a little at a time, folding just till blended. Wash beaters. Beat egg whites with cream of tartar till soft peaks form. Gradually add remaining ½ cup sugar, beating till stiff peaks form. Thoroughly but gently fold yolk mixture into whites. Bake the cake in an *ungreased* 10-inch tube pan at 325° about 55 minutes. Invert cake in pan; cool.

## Almond Brittle Torte

**1½ cups sifted all-purpose flour**
**¾ cup sugar**
**8 egg yolks**
**¼ cup cold water**
**1 tablespoon lemon juice**
**1 teaspoon vanilla**
**8 egg whites**
**1 teaspoon cream of tartar**
**1 teaspoon salt**

• • •

**¾ cup sugar**
**½ teaspoon instant coffee powder**
**2 tablespoons light corn syrup**
**2 tablespoons water**
**1½ teaspoons *sifted* baking soda**

• • •

**2 cups whipping cream**
**1 tablespoon sugar**
**2 teaspoons vanilla**
**½ cup toasted almond halves**

*To make sponge cake:* Sift flour and ¾ cup sugar into mixing bowl. Make well in center; add egg yolks, ¼ cup water, lemon juice, and 1 teaspoon vanilla. Beat till batter is smooth.

Beat egg whites with cream of tartar and salt till very soft peaks form; add ¾ cup sugar gradually, two tablespoons at a time. Continue beating till stiff peaks form. Fold egg yolk batter gently into egg white meringue.

Pour batter into an *ungreased* 10-inch tube pan. Carefully cut through batter, going around the tube 5 or 6 times with knife to break large air bubbles. Bake at 350° till top springs back when touched lightly, about 50 to 55 minutes. Invert pan; cool.

*To make almond brittle topping:* While cake bakes, mix ¾ cup sugar, coffee powder, corn syrup, and 2 tablespoons water in a saucepan. Cook to soft-crack stage (285° to 290°). Remove from heat; add soda at once. Stir vigorously, but only till mixture blends and pulls away from pan. Pour into buttered 8x8x2-inch pan. *Do not spread or stir.* Cool. Tap bottom of pan to remove candy. Crush into coarse crumbs.

*To assemble torte:* Remove cake from pan and split crosswise in 4 equal layers. Whip cream with 1 tablespoon sugar and 2 teaspoons vanilla; spread *half* between cake layers and the remainder over top and sides. Sprinkle surface with candy crumbs. Trim with almond halves by inserting them porcupine-style all over cake.

**Sponge cakemaking tip**

Remember to wash beaters and bowl used for egg yolks before using them to whip whites. Any trace of fat from the yolks will prevent the egg whites from whipping properly.

Numerous serving possibilities are yours with a sponge cake. Dust it with confectioners' sugar, or frost it, top it with ice cream and sweetened fruit, or use it as the basis for elegant desserts such as an Almond Brittle Torte.

By varying the ingredients or mixing techniques, you can produce many cake versions of excellent volume and flavor. Although originally sponge cakes did not contain leavening other than the air whipped into the egg whites today, baking powder is commonly used to ensure good volume in the finished cake. Likewise, foam cakes by definition do not contain shortening, but there are delicious versions of sponge cake that count small amounts of butter—for flavor and tenderness—among their list of ingredients.

Not all sponge cakes are the tall, tube cakes. For example, the practical and versatile Hot Milk Sponge Cake is baked in a square pan or a single-layer cake pan. Other variations include ladyfingers—which are actually miniature sponge cakes baked in special pans—and jelly rolls, which are made from sponge cake batter baked in large, flat pans. (See also *Cake*.)

Create a luscious dessert by spreading whipped cream atop and between slices of golden sponge cake. Crushed candy and almonds add the finishing touches to Almond Brittle Torte.

### Pineapple Fluff Cake

**6 egg yolks**
**½ cup pineapple juice**
**1 tablespoon lemon juice**
**1½ cups sifted cake flour**
**1 teaspoon baking powder**
**¾ cup sugar**
**6 egg whites**
**¼ teaspoon salt**
**¾ cup sugar**

Beat egg yolks till thick and lemon-colored. Add pineapple and lemon juices; beat till well combined. Sift cake flour, baking powder, and ¾ cup sugar together twice. Add to egg yolk mixture. Wash the beaters.

Beat egg whites with salt till soft peaks form; gradually add remaining ¾ cup sugar, beating till stiff peaks form. Fold batter into egg whites. Bake in *ungreased* 10-inch tube pan at 325° about 1 hour. Invert; cool.

### Hot Milk Sponge Cake

**1 cup sifted all-purpose flour**
**1 teaspoon baking powder**
**¼ teaspoon salt**
**½ cup milk**
**2 tablespoons butter**
**2 eggs**
**1 cup sugar**
**1 teaspoon vanilla**

Sift together flour, baking powder, and salt. Heat milk and butter till butter melts; keep hot. Beat eggs till thick and lemon-colored, 3 minutes on high speed of electric mixer. Gradually add sugar, beating constantly at medium speed for 4 to 5 minutes. Add sifted dry ingredients to egg mixture; stir just till blended. Slowly stir in hot milk mixture and vanilla; blend well. Turn into greased and floured 9x9x2-inch baking pan. Bake at 350° for 25 to 30 minutes. Do not invert. Cool in pan.

**SPOON**—**1.** A wooden, metal, or plastic implement consisting of a small, shallow bowl with a handle, used for cooking or eating. It is useful for stirring, creaming, and transferring foods. **2.** The act of transferring a mixture using a spoon.

**SPOON BREAD**—A baked cornmeal mixture the consistency of porridge. Spoon bread, a popular dish in the South, is served warm topped with butter in place of rice or potatoes with the main course.

### Spoon Bread

**1 cup cornmeal**
**3 cups milk**
**1 teaspoon salt**
**1 teaspoon baking powder**
**2 tablespoons salad oil**
**3 well-beaten egg yolks**
**3 stiffly beaten egg whites**

Cook cornmeal and *2 cups* of the milk till the consistency of mush; remove from heat. Add salt, baking bowder, oil, and remaining milk. Add well-beaten yolks; fold in stiffly beaten egg whites. Bake in a greased 2-quart casserole at 325° about 1 hour. Makes 6 servings.

**SPRAT**—A small, saltwater fish related to the herring. Sprats are also called brisling and are used as sardines. They live along the coasts of Europe and grow to a maximum of five inches in length.

Sprats are sold fresh, canned, pickled, and smoked. (See *Herring*, *Sardine* for additional information.)

**SPREAD**—**1.** Any food or mixture of foods that is soft enough to be distributed over the surface of a food such as bread or crackers with a knife or spatula. **2.** To distribute butter, frosting, filling, or mixture over the surface of a food.

Spreadable mixtures take many forms. Butter, margarine, peanut butter, and jam are popular spreads for bread. So are soft cheeses, deviled ham, seafood mixtures, and many sandwich fillings or canapé toppings. Appetizer spreads are sometimes packed into a small, buttered bowl or mold. When chilled, the mixture sets up enough to retain the shape of the mold but stays soft enough so that guests can spread it easily on crisp crackers or toast rounds. Smoothing a frosting over top and sides of a cake and buttering bread or toast are examples of spreading techniques.

## Clam Spread

*A peppy seafood appetizer spread flecked with bits of chopped, unpeeled cucumber—*

**1 7½-ounce can minced clams**
**1 clove garlic**
**1 8-ounce package cream cheese, softened**
**1 teaspoon lemon juice**
**1 teaspoon Worcestershire sauce**
**¼ teaspoon salt**
**Dash pepper**
**½ cup finely chopped, unpeeled cucumber**
**Snipped parsley**

Drain clams, reserving 1 tablespoon liquid. Rub mixing bowl with cut clove of garlic. In bowl blend clams, clam liquid, and next 6 ingredients. Chill. Turn into a serving bowl; sprinkle with parsley. Makes 1½ cups.

## Crab and Cheese Spread

**1 6-ounce package smoky cheese spread**
**1 3-ounce can deviled crab spread**
**¼ cup chopped pimiento-stuffed green olives**
**2 teaspoons milk**

Combine all ingredients in a bowl. Blend thoroughly with electric mixer. Spread mixture on melba toast or unsalted crackers, or stuff mixture into celery sections. Makes 1¼ cups.

## Zesty Chicken Spread

**1 5-ounce can chicken spread**
**2 tablespoons mayonnaise or salad dressing**
**1½ teaspoons prepared horseradish**
**¾ teaspoon Worcestershire sauce**
**¼ teaspoon dry mustard**
**¼ cup chopped almonds, toasted**
**1 tablespoon milk**

Blend all ingredients. Chill. Thin with additional milk, if desired. Spread on crackers or party rye bread slices. Garnish with crisp bacon, if desired. Makes ¾ cup spread.

## Ham Salad Sandwich Spread

*A blender-quick way to use leftover ham—*

Put ½ cup mayonnaise; 1 large sweet pickle; 1 small stalk celery, sliced; and ½ teaspoon prepared mustard in blender. Blend till pickle and celery are chopped. Add 1½ cups cubed, fully cooked ham, ½ cup at a time. Blend after each addition to chop ham. Chill. Makes 1⅔ cups.

## Olive-Cheese Ball

**1 8-ounce package cream cheese, softened**
**4 ounces blue cheese**
**¼ cup butter, softened**
**½ cup chopped, pitted, ripe olives well drained**
**1 tablespoon snipped chives**
**¼ cup chopped walnuts**

Cream together cheeses and butter. Stir in olives and chives. Chill slightly. Form into ball. Chill thoroughly. Press nuts into ball. Trim with parsley, if desired. Makes 2½ cups.

**SPRIG**—In cooking, a small shoot or leafy twig of fresh herb or plant used in a bouquet garni or to decorate food. Mint and parsley sprigs are the most familiar examples. (See also *Bouquet Garni.*)

An Olive-Cheese Ball is one of the best cracker spreads ever. Flavor and spreadability come from blue and cream cheeses.

**SPRINGERLE** ***(shpring' uhr lē)*** – A thick, hard, anise-flavored cookie with a raised design made by pressing rolled dough with a carved block or rolling pin. The cookies are a German Christmas tradition.

The carved blocks or rolling pins used for making the cookies may have simple or intricate patterns, depending on the skills of the craftsman. Trees, people, stylized flowers, or Christmas designs are popular patterns. Many old, beautifully carved molds hold places of honor in museum collections of cooking utensils.

Because of the square corners on the molds, the finished cookies are square or rectangular in shape. A sharp knife is used to cut the cookies apart before baking. Baking time is watched carefully so that the cookies are not brown when done, but emerge from the oven a delicate yellow color. (See also *Christmas*.)

Beautiful, hand-carved blocks are used to imprint the design on Springerle, an anise-flavored Christmas cookie from Germany.

## Springerle

- **4 eggs**
- **1 pound sifted confectioners' sugar (about 4 cups)**
- **20 drops anise oil**
- **4 cups sifted all-purpose flour**
- **1 teaspoon baking soda**
- **Crushed aniseed**

With electric mixer, beat eggs till light. Gradually add sugar; continue beating on high speed till mixture is like soft meringue, 15 minutes. Add anise oil. Sift together flour and soda; blend into mixture at low speed. Cover bowl with foil; let stand 15 minutes.

Divide dough in thirds. On lightly floured surface, roll each piece in an 8-inch square, a little more than ¼ inch thick. Let stand 1 minute. Lightly dust springerle rolling pin or mold with flour; roll or press hard enough to make a clear design. With sharp knife, cut cookies apart. Place on floured surface; cover with a towel and let stand overnight.

Grease cookie sheets and sprinkle with 1½ to 2 teaspoons crushed aniseed. Brush excess flour from cookies; with finger, rub underside of each cookie very lightly with cold water and place on cookie sheets. Bake at 300° till light straw color, about 20 minutes. Makes 6 dozen cookies. Store in airtight container.

Springerle can also be imprinted by using a specially carved rolling pin on which the designs are marked off into squares. After rolling the pin over the dough, use a sharp knife to separate the cookies.

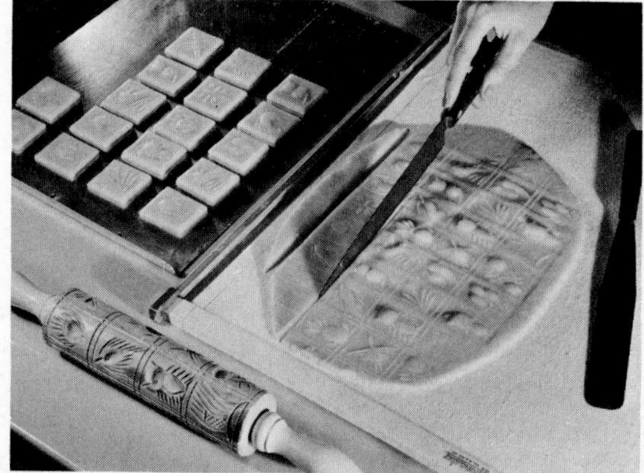

**SPRINGFORM PAN**—A straight-sided, round baking pan in two sections held together with a spring latch. When food is to be removed, the latch is opened and the sides lifted off leaving the food on the bottom section. A springform pan is used for cheesecakes and other desserts that would not lift out intact from a standard pan. This Strawberry-Rhubarb Cheesecake uses a springform pan to advantage.

## Strawberry-Rhubarb Cheesecake

**1½ cups zwieback crumbs**
**⅓ cup sugar**
**¾ teaspoon ground cinnamon**
**6 tablespoons butter, melted**
**3 well-beaten eggs**
**2 8-ounce packages cream cheese, softened**
**1 cup sugar**
**2 teaspoons vanilla**
**½ teaspoon ground nutmeg**
**¼ teaspoon salt**
**3 cups dairy sour cream**
**1 cup fresh rhubarb, cut in 1-inch pieces (¼ pound)**
**⅓ cup sugar**
**1 tablespoon cornstarch**
**Dash salt**
**Red food coloring**
**2 cups fresh strawberries, halved**

Combine first 4 ingredients. Mix till crumbly; press onto bottom and about 1½ inches up sides of buttered 9-inch springform pan. Chill.

Combine next 6 ingredients; beat smooth. Blend in sour cream. Pour into crust. Bake at 375° just till set, about 40 to 45 minutes. Filling will be soft. Cool to room temperature.

In small saucepan combine rhubarb, ⅓ cup sugar, and ½ cup water. Bring to boiling; reduce heat. Simmer, uncovered, till almost tender, about 1 minute, being careful not to break up rhubarb. Remove from heat. Drain, reserving syrup. Add water if necessary to make ¾ cup. Mix cornstarch, dash salt, and 2 tablespoons cold water; add to syrup mixture. Cook and stir till thickened and bubbly; cook 1 minute more. Remove from heat; stir in 7 or 8 drops food coloring. Cool to room temperature. Arrange strawberries and rhubarb on cheesecake; spoon glaze over. Chill. Serves 12.

Unlatch the clamps on a springform pan to release the sides before lifting the top section away from cheesecake or dessert.

**SPRINKLE**—To scatter drops of liquid, crumbs, seasonings, or fine particles of one food lightly over another food.

**SPRING LAMB**—A designation for a lamb marketed during spring, summer, and early fall. The term, also known as genuine spring lamb, is used to distinguish this year's lambs from last year's.

Spring lamb is tender meat that is prized for its delicate flavor. Most shoulder, leg, and rib cuts can be cooked by dry heat in an oven, a broiler, or on an outdoor grill. Sometimes, however, very lean chops or cubed lamb are braised. (See also *Lamb*.)

## Lamb Chops Supreme

In large skillet slowly brown 6 shoulder or sirloin lamb chops, ½ inch thick, in small amount of hot shortening. Season with salt and pepper. Drain off fat. Add one 10½-ounce can condensed consommé; ½ cup chopped celery; ½ cup sliced green onion with tops; and ½ teaspoon dried thyme leaves, crushed. Cover; simmer till meat is tender, about 40 to 45 minutes.

Stack chops to one side. Drain one 3-ounce can broiled, chopped mushrooms, reserving liquid. Blend liquid into 3 tablespoons all-purpose flour. Gradually stir flour mixture into consommé in skillet; cook and stir till thickened and bubbly. Add mushrooms and 1 tablespoon dried parsley flakes; heat through. Serves 6.

**SPRITZ, SPRITS**—A rich, Scandinavian butter cookie that is shaped by forcing soft dough through a cookie press. Sometimes, the dough for spritz cookies is tinted or the cookies are sprinkled with colored sugars before they are baked.

Although not difficult to use, a cookie press takes patience and practice. Be sure to follow the press manufacturer's directions carefully. It is important that the disk is placed in the press so that the cutting edge will be against the dough, thus, releasing the cookie easily after pressing. Another hint that works with many types of cookie presses is to give the handle a reverse half turn after pressing each of the cookies onto the cookie sheet.

The cookie press comes equipped with several disks, each producing a different design. The designs usually include a ribbon, Christmas tree, star, or perhaps a camel. Rings and wreaths can be made by pressing the dough in a long, slender ribbon, cutting the ribbon into four-inch strips and shaping easily into a circle.

## Spritz

**1½ cups butter or margarine**
**1 cup sugar**
**1 egg**
**1 teaspoon vanilla**
**½ teaspoon almond extract**
**4 cups sifted all-purpose flour**
**1 teaspoon baking powder**

Thoroughly cream butter and sugar. Add egg, vanilla, and almond extract; beat well. Sift together flour and baking powder; add gradually to creamed mixture, mixing to smooth dough. Do not chill the dough.

Force dough through cookie press onto *ungreased* cookie sheet. Bake at 400° about 8 minutes; cool. Makes 6 dozen cookies.

***For perfectly shaped spritz cookies***

Be sure to let the cookie sheet cool between batches of cookies. Dough pressed onto a hot cookie sheet will melt out of shape.

**SPUMONI, SPUMONE** ***(spuh mō' nē)***—A multilayered Italian ice cream This rainbow-hued frozen dessert is composed of strips of ice cream of various flavors and colors packed into a mold. Pieces of nuts or fruits may be incorporated into one or more of the layers. At serving time, the ice cream is unmolded and sliced across the layers so that each serving contains a strip of each color.

The basic ice cream mixture is rich. Each layer contributes its own flavor and color to a beautiful and delectable dessert. While there is a certain degree of latitude in the number of layers, a creamy, chocolate, a green, and a pink layer are fairly typical. The creamy layer is often flavored with rum, which gives spumoni an almost eggnog quality. The chocolate layer may be ice cream or a smooth chocolaty-flavored whipped cream mixture.

The green layer gets its characteristic flavor from finely chopped pistachio nuts. Even when almonds are substituted, the layer is still tinted green. The pink layer derives its color and flavor from the fruit, often strawberries or raspberries, used to prepare it. The color can be deepened, if desired, by adding a few drops of red food coloring before piling into the mold.

Commercially made spumoni is frequently packed in rectangular cartons, which make the frozen dessert easy to slice. However, when preparing spumoni at home, you can create a more spectacular effect by using a two-quart metal or heatproof glass mixing bowl for the mold. Attractive, wedge-shaped portions show off the colored layers to the best advantage.

Although spumoni is a time-consuming dessert to prepare because time must be allowed for each layer to freezer before the next one is added, the finished mold is a work of art and well worth every minute spent. (See *Ice Cream, Italian Cookery* for additional information.)

***An Italian spectacular***

Gather compliments galore with colorful → Italian Spumoni. Trim the elegant ice cream mold with tinted whipped cream.

## Italian Spumoni

**1½ pints French vanilla ice cream**
**1 teaspoon rum flavoring**
**6 candied *or* maraschino cherries**
**1½ pints French vanilla ice cream**
**½ teaspoon almond flavoring**
**Few drops green food coloring**
**⅓ cup finely chopped, unblanched almond *or* pistachio nuts**

. . .

**¾ cup whipping cream**
**⅓ cup instant cocoa powder mix**

. . .

**1 10-ounce package frozen red raspberries, thawed**
**¾ cup whipping cream**
**⅓ cup sifted confectioners' sugar**
**Few drops red food coloring**

*To make eggnog layer:* For mold, chill a 2-quart metal or glass bowl in the freezer. In another mixing bowl stir in 1½ pints ice cream just to soften; stir in rum flavoring. Refreeze only till workable. With chilled spoon, spread quickly in layer over bottom and sides of the *previously chilled* bowl, being sure ice cream comes all the way to top. (If ice cream tends to slip, refreeze in bowl till workable.) Circle cherries in bottom of bowl. Freeze till firm.

*To make pistachio layer:* Stir remaining 1½ pints ice cream just to soften; stir in almond flavoring, green food coloring, and nuts. Refreeze only till workable. Quickly spread over inside of first layer. Freeze till firm.

*To make chocolate layer:* Combine ¾ cup whipping cream and cocoa; whip till peaks hold. Quickly spread over pistachio layer. Return to freezer; freeze till firm.

*To make raspberry layer:* Drain berries (do not use syrup); sieve berries. Mix together ½ *cup* of the whipping cream, confectioners' sugar, and dash salt; whip to soft peaks. Fold in sieved berries. (Add a few drops red food coloring, if needed.) Pile into center of mold; smooth top. Cover the mold tightly with foil. Freeze 6 hours or overnight.

*To serve:* Whip remaining cream; tint pink. Peel off foil. Invert on *chilled* plate. To loosen, rub bowl with towel wrung out in hot water; lift off bowl. Trim with pink-tinted whipped cream piped on with pastry tube. Add frosted grapes, if desired. Cut spumoni in small wedges. Makes 12 to 16 servings.

### *How to pack spumoni*

Stir vanilla ice cream to soften. Blend in flavoring. Spread ice cream up sides of large mixing bowl or mold. Freeze firm.

Working quickly, spread pistachio layer inside mold. Freeze. Repeat with other layers, freezing mold after each addition.

Freeze Spumoni firm—six hours or overnight. To serve, invert mold on *chilled* platter and use a hot towel to loosen ice cream.

**SPROUT, SPROUTS**–**1.** The edible shoot of certain plants. **2.** With "s" added, a colloquial word for brussels sprouts that is occasionally applied also to bean sprouts. (See *Bean Sprouts, Brussels Sprouts* for additional information.)

**SPUN SUGAR**–Sugar syrup, plain or colored, that is boiled to the long-thread stage then quickly drawn, a little at a time, into long threads. The hot syrup is dropped in a thin stream from a special implement, back and forth between two bars. Strands harden quickly but can be bunched and shaped into nests or rosettes, which are often used to hold ice cream or as decorations for fancy desserts.

**SQUAB**–A young pigeon, not more than four weeks old, weighing about one pound. Although squab are difficult to locate, ready-to-cook birds are marketed frozen. If there is a hunter in your family, you may have wild squab to enjoy.

Through the centuries, these young pigeons have been on the menu for gigantic feasts and humbler family fare alike. They were roasted for diners' pleasure at Roman banquets, and, as cooking became more sophisticated over the years, they were sauced or stuffed with forcemeat before being presented at the tables. Cooks doing their marketing in London in 1272 found pigeons selling three for a penny.

In America, during colonial times and in the movement of pioneers westward, pigeons were among the native food supply. During migration of the birds, rural families, city dwellers, and travelers ate the tender meat daily in some form. The passenger pigeon was one of the major species used for food. The supply seemed inexhaustible at that time, but, this was not the case. By 1914 the species was extinct.

Today, squab, though not so plentiful, is nonetheless delicious when available and cooked properly. Because the meat is tender, the birds can be fried or roasted on a spit. Stuffing and roasting is another popular method of preparation. Since there is little internal fat in the young squab, it is delicious cut up and cooked in a seasoned sauce, which preserves juiciness and adds flavor. (See also *Game.*)

## Savory Squab

**4 12- to 14-ounce ready-to-cook squab, split lengthwise**
**2 tablespoons butter or margarine**
**1 tablespoon finely chopped onion**
**1½ teaspoons chicken-flavored gravy base**
**¼ cup dry sherry**
**2 teaspoons cornstarch**

Brown squab in butter in large skillet about 10 minutes. Add onion, gravy base, ½ cup water, and dash pepper; bring to boiling. Simmer, covered, till tender, about 30 minutes. Remove squab to warm serving platter. Skim fat from sauce. Combine wine and cornstarch; blend with mixture in skillet. Cook and stir until mixture thickens and bubbles. Serve sauce over squab. Makes 4 servings.

## Squab on a Spit

**2 12- to 14-ounce ready-to-cook squab**
**¼ cup currant jelly**
**1 teaspoon prepared mustard**

Mount squab on spit. Attach spit to rotisserie in broiler and broil for 45 minutes. Brush occasionally with Currant Glaze the last 15 minutes of cooking time. Makes 2 servings.

*Currant Glaze:* Combine currant jelly and mustard in small saucepan; heat, stirring until jelly melts and sauce is heated.

## Sweet-Sour Squab

**4 12- to 14-ounce ready-to-cook squab, split in quarters**
**¼ cup butter or margarine**
**¼ cup sliced green onions**
**¼ cup tarragon vinegar**
**1 tablespoon sugar**
**¼ teaspoon salt**

Brown squab on all sides in butter in large skillet. Add onion and cook until tender but not brown. Combine vinegar, sugar, and salt; add to skillet. Cover and simmer until tender, about 30 to 35 minutes. Remove squab to platter and serve. Makes 4 servings.

# SQUASH

***Shapely, colorful, and nutritious, these vegetables add seasonal splendor to a meal.***

Many foods commonly cooked in America today are descendants of the American Indian dishes. Squash is just one of these foods. The Indians named squash *askutasquash,* which means "eating raw or uncooked." Although this may be the manner in which they used squash, our tastes have developed a preference for it cooked.

Squash, along with muskmelons, watermelons, cucumbers, and pumpkins, belongs to the gourd family. The plants of this family are all vine-growing and are characterized by large leaves and tendrils that attach to other objects for support.

This vegetable is classified into two main groups—summer and winter squash—according to how fast the squash grows and at what stage it is harvested. Within these groups, there are numerous varieties that differ from one another in size, shape, color, and texture. Some are about the size of a cucumber; others, as big as a watermelon. The varietal names are often indicative of their shape—acorn, turban, and crookneck, for example. Skin colors are light to dark green and yellow to bright orange. One variety of squash even has a blue cast. Textures vary from crisp and moist to soft and dry.

Like tomatoes and kidney beans, squash are native to the Western Hemisphere. They have been utilized and cultivated by Indians for centuries—first by the South American and later by Central and North American tribes. The earliest cultivators raised squash primarily for the edible seeds since it was the seeds rather than the pulp that made up the largest portion of these early squash varieties. During the settlement of Virginia, Capt. John Smith found the Indians raising and eating a squash variety that they called *macocks.* Not until the latter part of the 1500s, however, did European explorers take squash back to their homelands. In areas such as Italy, squash became so popular that these people developed several varieties of their own, such as zucchini. In northern Europe, squash plants did not thrive as well as they did in the south.

***How squash are produced:*** In the United States, squash are grown both commercially and in home gardens. In colder regions, the plants must be cultivated as annuals since they are quite susceptible to freezing temperatures, while in areas where warm temperatures remain year round, squash are perennials. They prefer light, sandy, yet fairly rich soil.

Squash seeds are planted in "hills." (These are not mounds as the name implies, but depressed areas where water collects during a rainfall.) To get a head start on the growing season in the north, plants are sometimes started indoors a few weeks before the last winter frost. Some other varieties are seeded outdoors and mature in a short growing season.

Squash harvest time depends on the variety of squash. Summer squash are picked a few days after they develop so that the rinds and seeds are still tender. Winter squash varieties are allowed to fully mature on the vines and are picked before the first frost of winter. Even though the rinds are hard, winter squash must be picked carefully to avoid bruises.

### *Squash in profusion*

← From the arrival of summer to the passing of autumn, there's an array of fresh squash varieties harvested to suit every taste.

## Summer squash

These quick-growing vegetables are so soft-shelled and seeded that they can be eaten shell and all. Choose one of the many varieties to highlight your meals.

***Nutritional value:*** Summer squash have a higher percentage of water than do their winter relatives. One-half cup of cooked summer squash adds only 15 calories to a meal while providing a fair amount of vitamin A and the B vitamin niacin. Moderate amounts of vitamin C are present too.

***Types of summer squash:*** Because the shape, size, and color of each variety is so diverse, squash are easy to identify. A description of the summer squash most frequently used follows:

*Chayote* is pear-shaped and about acorn squash size. The rind is soft and pale green; the inner flesh is tinged with green, too. This variety has a single, large seed that is soft enough to eat.

*Crookneck* has a curved or straight neck and a bulging base. The yellow rind is bumpy; the pulp is yellow and grainy.

*Cymling, Scallop, or Pattypan* develops into a scallop-edge disk. The smooth or slightly rough skin is green when young but increasingly whitens as it matures. The interior flesh is green-tinged. There is also a yellow form.

*Italian or Zucchini,* first cultivated in Italy, is shaped like a straight cylinder that graduates to a slightly larger size at the blossom end. The skin is dark green and is speckled with pale yellow, stripelike markings. The greenish-white flesh is very fine.

***Squash seeds as food***

Although South Americans relish the taste of squash as much as North Americans, they also make good use of the seeds. Sometimes the seeds are roasted and eaten like peanuts. Or, the shelled seeds are ground for use in sauces. Squash seeds ground to a paste and sweetened are even the basic ingredient for specially molded and decorated confections.

***How to select and store:*** Although fresh summer squash are available during a major portion of the year in some localities, the peak crops are marketed during the summer. Some summer varieties are also available in the frozen state.

In selecting summer squash, the more immature the squash, the better. Choose squash that are heavy for their size, firm well-formed, and glossy. The rinds should be fresh-looking according to the variety. Avoid hard and dull-rinded squash.

Because of their immaturity, summer squash do not keep well. Refrigerate them in the vegetable crisper for short periods only. For best flavor and texture, use summer squash as soon as possible.

***How to prepare:*** Because the rinds and seeds of summer squash are tender they are not removed when cooked. To prepare the squash for eating, wash but do not peel. Cut off the stem and blossom ends.

The squash may be left whole or be halved, sliced, or cubed as desired. (Cut Chayote squash right through the seed.)

The texture of summer squash is best when slightly crisp so that the pieces retain their shape. For slices and cubes, cook, covered, in a small amount of boiling, salted water for 8 to 15 minutes.

***How to use:*** For lightly seasoned summer squash, salt, pepper, a dash sugar, and butter are usually added to the cooking liquid. If you wish, simply stir-fry squash slices in sizzling seasoned butter. Other flavorings used to enhance the delicateness of summer squash include beef or chicken bouillon cubes, Parmesan cheese, basil, bay leaf, mace, marjoram, mustard, and rosemary. Vegetable combinations using summer squash are popular, too—tomatoes, onion, and green pepper are typical ingredients used with summer squash.

Whole or halved summer squash perform a dual role as vegetable and serving dish when filled with a savory stuffing. Try different stuffing mixtures based on another vegetable, meat, or bread.

Summer squash need not always be cooked before eating. Marinate uncooked slices in a piquant salad dressing, or use the raw pieces in a lettuce or meat salad.

## Savory Vegetable Trio

**½ pound fresh green beans, cut up**
**½ cup chopped onion**
**¼ cup snipped parsley**
**1 teaspoon salt**
**¼ teaspoon dried thyme leaves, crushed**
**¼ teaspoon ground sage**
**⅛ teaspoon pepper**
**2 cups cubed yellow summer squash**
**3 large tomatoes, peeled and cut in wedges**
**2 tablespoons butter or margarine**

In saucepan combine beans, onion, parsley, salt, thyme, sage, pepper, and ½ cup water. Bring to boiling. Cover; reduce heat and simmer 10 minutes. Add squash; simmer, covered, till vegetables are tender, about 10 minutes more. Drain. Add tomatoes and butter; cover and heat through. Makes 6 servings.

## Summer Squash Skillet

**½ cup chopped onion**
**½ cup chopped green pepper**
**2 tablespoons butter or margarine**
**1 tablespoon sugar**
**1 teaspoon all-purpose flour**
**1 teaspoon salt**
**¼ teaspoon pepper**
**2 cups cubed pattypan squash (about ¾ pound)**
**3 medium tomatoes, peeled and cut in wedges**

Cook onion and green pepper in butter till tender; stir in sugar, flour, salt, and pepper. Add squash and tomatoes. Cook over low heat just till vegetables are tender. Serves 4 to 6.

Zucchini squash has become one of the most popular of the summer squash varieties. A crisp texture and mild flavor are its decidingly appealing characteristics. Coupled with zippy cheeses or with fresh vegetables such as tomatoes and mushrooms, a pleasing texture and color contrast is achieved. Add zucchini slices to scrambled eggs, then sprinkle with Parmesan cheese for a delicious and easy supper.

## Zucchini Sweet-Sour Medley

**2 tablespoons salad oil**
**4 teaspoons cornstarch**
**1 tablespoon sugar**
**1 tablespoon instant minced onion**
**2 teaspoons prepared mustard**
**¾ teaspoon salt**
**½ teaspoon garlic salt**
**Dash pepper**

• • •

**½ cup water**
**¼ cup vinegar**
**4 cups bias-sliced zucchini squash (3 or 4 zucchini)**
**1 cup bias-sliced celery**

• • •

**2 tomatoes, quartered**

In a medium skillet stir together salad oil, cornstarch, sugar, instant minced onion, prepared mustard, salt, garlic salt, and pepper. Add water and vinegar to seasoning mixture; cook and stir till mixture thickens and bubbles.

Add zucchini and celery; cook, covered, till vegetables are crisp-tender, about 7 to 8 minutes. Stir occasionally. Add tomatoes and cook the mixture, covered, till heated through, 2 to 3 minutes more. Makes 6 servings.

Brown sugar-glazed apples spiced with ginger are mounded in acorn squash halves to give Apple-Filled Squash their golden glow.

## Skillet Squash

**2 medium zucchini squash**
**1 medium onion**
**2 teaspoons butter or margarine**
**½ teaspoon salt**
**Dash coarsely ground pepper**
• • •
**1 medium tomato, cut in wedges**
**1 2-ounce can sliced mushrooms, drained**

Scrub squash in cold water; cut off ends. Cut into thin, crosswise slices (about 2 cups). Thinly slice onion and separate into rings. Melt the 2 teaspoons butter in a 12-inch skillet; add salt and pepper. Cook onion in butter till crisp-tender. Add the squash.

Cover and cook 6 minutes, stirring occasionally. Add tomato and mushrooms. Continue cooking, covered, till tomato and mushrooms are heated through and squash is crisp-tender, about 4 minutes. Remove to serving bowl with slotted spoon. Makes 6 servings.

## Saucy Zucchini

*Has a cheese and buttered crumb topping—*

**1 pound zucchini squash, thinly sliced (about 4 cups)**
**2 medium onions, thinly sliced (about 1 cup)**
**2 tablespoons butter or margarine**
**2 tablespoons all-purpose flour**
**1 teaspoon salt**
**Dash pepper**
**1 cup milk**
• • •
**2 ounces sharp process American cheese, shredded (½ cup)**
**½ cup buttered bread crumbs**

Cook zucchini and onion in small amount boiling water till tender. In a saucepan melt butter; blend in flour, salt, and pepper. Add the milk all at once; cook, stirring constantly, until mixture thickens and bubbles. Combine the sauce with the cooked vegetables.

Place the mixture in a 10x6x1¾-inch baking dish. Top with shredded cheese and then with buttered crumbs. Bake at 350° for about 25 minutes. Makes 4 to 6 servings.

## Zucchini Florentine

*Sliced squash bakes in a well-seasoned custard—*

**6 small zucchini squash, cut in ¼-inch slices**
**2 tablespoons butter or margarine**
• • •
**1 cup evaporated milk**
**3 slightly beaten eggs**
**1 teaspoon salt**
**¼ teaspoon garlic salt**
**¼ teaspoon pepper**
• • •
**¼ teaspoon paprika**

Place zucchini in a 1½-quart casserole; dot with butter. Bake at 400° till zucchini is partially cooked but still crisp, about 15 minutes. Combine milk, eggs, salt, garlic salt, and pepper; pour over zucchini. Sprinkle with paprika. Set casserole in a shallow pan, filling pan to 1 inch with hot water.

Bake at 350° till a knife inserted halfway between center and edge comes out clean, about 40 minutes. Makes 6 servings.

## Cheese-Sauced Zucchini Fritters

*A deluxe side dish—*

**1½ cups sifted all-purpose flour**
**2 teaspoons baking powder**
**¾ teaspoon salt**
**1 cup milk**
**1 beaten egg**
**1 cup finely chopped zucchini squash**
**Cheese Sauce**

Stir together flour, baking powder, and salt. Combine milk, egg, and zucchini; add to dry ingredients and mix just till moistened. Drop from tablespoon into deep, hot fat (375°). Fry, a few at a time, for 3 or 4 minutes; drain. Spoon Cheese Sauce over. Makes 24 fritters.

*Cheese Sauce:* Melt 2 tablespoons butter or margarine; blend in 2 tablespoons all-purpose flour, ¼ teaspoon salt, and dash pepper. Add 1¼ cups milk all at once. Cook and stir till thickened and bubbly. Add ½ cup shredded sharp process American cheese and ½ cup shredded process Swiss cheese; stir till melted.

### Zucchini, Chinese-Style

**2 slices bacon**
**3 medium zucchini squash, scored and sliced diagonally**
**1/4 cup chicken broth**
• • •
**2 teaspoons cornstarch**
**1/2 teaspoon salt**
**2 teaspoons cold water**

Cook bacon till crisp; remove from skillet. Add sliced zucchini to bacon drippings in skillet; toss to coat. Pour chicken broth over zucchini. Cover and steam till squash is almost tender, about 4 to 5 minutes.

Blend cornstarch and salt with cold water; stir into zucchini mixture. Cook, stirring constantly, till mixture bubbles. Turn into serving dish; garnish with crisp-cooked, crumbled bacon. Makes 4 or 5 servings.

### Zucchini with Walnuts

**1 pound zucchini squash, cut in 1/2-inch slices**
**1/3 cup sliced green onion**
**2 tablespoons butter or margarine**
**2 tablespoons dry sherry**
**1/2 teaspoon salt**
**1/4 cup walnut halves**

In medium saucepan combine zucchini slices, green onion, and butter. Cook, uncovered, over low heat for 5 minutes. Stir in sherry and salt; cover and cook over low heat till vegetables are tender, 5 minutes more. Stir in walnuts; serve immediately. Serves 5 or 6.

### Zucchini Supreme

**4 cups sliced zucchini squash**
**1 medium onion, thinly sliced and separated into rings**
**3 medium tomatoes, peeled and sliced**
**1/2 cup chopped green pepper**
**1 8-ounce package sliced process American cheese**
**3 cups 1/2-inch caraway rye bread cubes**
**1/4 cup butter or margarine, melted**

Alternate layers of zucchini, onion, tomato, and green pepper in 13½x8¾x1¾-inch baking dish; season. Cut cheese slices in half diagonally; place atop casserole. Sprinkle with bread cubes; drizzle with butter.

Cover and bake at 350° for 45 minutes; uncover and bake till tender, about 15 minutes longer. Makes 8 to 10 servings.

### Garden Vegetable Bowl

**1/4 cup butter or margarine**
**4 cups sliced zucchini squash (about 1 pound)**
**1½ cups cut fresh, frozen, *or* drained, canned whole kernel corn**
**1/2 cup chopped onion**
**1/3 cup chopped green pepper**
• • •
**1/2 teaspoon salt**
**1 tablespoon fresh, snipped dill *or* 1 teaspoon dried dillweed**

Melt butter in skillet; add zucchini, corn, onion, and green pepper. Sprinkle with salt. Cover and cook, stirring occasionally, till vegetables are tender, about 10 to 12 minutes. Sprinkle with dill. Serves 4 to 6.

For a menu change-of-pace, substitute Nutmeg Whipped Squash for the mashed potatoes. (See *Acorn Squash* for recipe.)

Thinly slice zucchini teams up with tomato wedges and sliced mushrooms in a simple version of buttery Skillet Squash.

### Steak and Zucchini Supper

**1 pound round steak, cut in thin strips**
**1 tablespoon salad oil**
**1 10½-ounce can mushroom gravy**
**½ cup water**
**½ envelope spaghetti sauce mix with mushrooms (about 2 tablespoons)**
**3 to 4 medium zucchini squash, cut in 1½-inch slices**
**Hot cooked noodles *or* rice**

In a skillet quickly brown steak strips in hot salad oil. Add gravy, water, and spaghetti sauce mix; stir till well combined. Cover; cook over low heat for about 20 minutes, stirring occasionally. Add zucchini slices. Cover and continue cooking till zucchini is crisp-tender, about 10 to 12 minutes. Serve over noodles or rice. Makes 4 servings.

## Winter squash

These are the late-harvested varieties most closely associated with the bounty of fall and Thanksgiving celebrations. The fully mature squash have hard rinds and seeds, neither of which is usually eaten.

***Nutritional value:*** The long growing season of winter squash enables many nutrients to build up in this vegetable. Winter squash contain more calories than do summer squash (63 calories for one-half cup baked squash). The vibrant yellow color of the pulp is indicative of its excellent contribution of vitamin A. Winter squash is considered also to be a fair source of the B vitamin riboflavin.

***Types of winter squash:*** The list of popular winter squash varieties is even more lengthy than the summer ones. These, too, are diverse in appearance and taste.

*Acorn, also called Des Moines, or Table Queen,* is one of the most popular of all squash varieties. It is easily identified by its acorn shape. Acorn squash usually varies from five to eight inches in length. The thin, smooth rind is a shiny deep green, parts of which change to orange and dull green in prolonged storage. The pale orange flesh turns to a brilliant yellow when cooked and is very tender, fairly dry, and sometimes fibrous.

*Banana* is elongated just as its name implies. This large squash often weighs as much as 12 pounds. The olive gray or creamy pink rind is fairly smooth and moderately thick. The light orange flesh is moderately dry and fine-textured.

*Butternut* may be 9 to 12 inches long with a cylindrical shape that is enlarged at the bottom third. The seed cavity is in this bulbous portion. The exterior is a light creamy brown or dark yellow, while the interior is orange and fine-textured.

*Delicata or Sweet Potato* is small like an acorn squash but oblong in shape. The thin rind is light yellow with green striping. The orange-colored pulp becomes tender and dry upon cooking.

*Delicious* is a top-shaped squash with the stem at the large end. It varies in length from 8 to 12 inches and in diameter from 8 to 10 inches. The slightly warted and ridged rind is dark green or bright orange-red, depending on the strain, and has stripes at the blossom end. The flesh is thick, yellow, and dry.

*Hubbard* has a globe shape and a fairly thick, tapered neck. The blossom end has a smaller taper. The bumpy, ridged rind may be dark bronze-green, blue-gray, or orange-red in color. The thick orange-yellow flesh is deliciously sweet.

*Turban* is turban-shaped at the blossom end. This large squash is 8 to 10 inches long and 12 to 15 inches in diameter. The extremely hard rind is thick and very warted. Probably the most colorful of squashes, its turban is blue and its base is a bright red-orange. The bright orange flesh cooks to a sweet, dry, and often fibrous product.

***How to select and store:*** Select winter squash that are heavy for their size, have hard rinds, and good coloring and shaping for the variety. Rinds that are soft or tender are immature and lack flavor and texture. Peak harvesting seasons are in the fall, but packages of frozen winter squash are available all year long.

Winter squash are more stable to store than summer squash. If handled carefully to prevent bruising, they can be kept many months in a cool, dry place. Any cuts or bruises result in rapid decay.

***How to prepare:*** Winter squash are usually washed, halved, and seeds and strings are removed before further treatment, although small varieties can be baked whole.

Small varieties, such as acorn squash, are left whole or are cut in halves or rings. Bake them in a shallow pan at 350°, cut sides down, for 35 to 40 minutes. Turn cut sides up and bake 20 to 25 minutes more. Cover the pan with foil the first half hour of baking to speed the cooking process. These squash may also be peeled, cubed, and cooked in a small amount of boiling, salted water. Cover and cook the squash till tender, about 15 minutes.

Large squash are either cut in serving-sized pieces or are peeled and cubed. Serving-sized pieces may be placed on a baking sheet, covered with foil, and baked at 350°. Hubbard squash requires about 1¼ hours of baking. When cooked, covered, in boiling, salted water, cubed squash should be done in 15 minutes.

***How to use:*** Most squash lovers enjoy this vegetable in pieces or mashed. When left in a serving-sized piece, winter squash can be filled with a meat stuffing for a main dish. Simply fill the cavity with butter and brown sugar or honey, and it becomes a side dish.

Mashed squash can be dressed up with butter, pineapple, marshmallows, nuts, or raisins. Try allspice, basil, chives, cinnamon, ginger, or oregano for seasoning. (See also *Vegetable*.)

## Apple-Filled Squash

**3 acorn squash**
**2 tablespoons butter or margarine, melted**
**1 18-ounce can pie-sliced apples**
**¾ cup brown sugar**
**1 teaspoon lemon juice**
**¼ teaspoon ground ginger**
**3 tablespoons butter or margarine**

Halve squash lengthwise; remove seeds. Brush with melted butter and sprinkle with a little salt. Place, cut side down, in large baking dish. Bake at 350° for 35 minutes. Combine apples, brown sugar, lemon juice, and ginger.

Turn squash, cut side up, in baking dish. Fill centers with apple mixture. Dot with butter. Continue baking till squash is tender, 25 minutes more. If desired, sprinkle with ground cinnamon before serving. Serves 6.

## Saucy Dilled Butternut

**4 cups peeled, cubed butternut squash (about 1½ pounds)**
**2 tablespoons sliced green onion with tops**
**1 tablespoon butter or margarine**
**½ cup dairy sour cream**
**2 tablespoons milk**
**½ teaspoon salt**
**Dash pepper**
**½ teaspoon dried dillweed**

In saucepan cook squash in boiling, salted water till tender, about 10 minutes; drain well. Cook green onion in butter till tender. Blend in sour cream, milk, salt, and pepper. Heat, *but do not boil.* Arrange squash on serving plate; top with sour cream mixture. Sprinkle with dillweed. Makes 4 to 6 servings.

## Squash Delight

**2 medium acorn squash**
**½ cup diced, fully cooked ham**
**2 tablespoons chopped green pepper**
**2 tablespoons chopped celery**
**2 tablespoons butter or margarine**
**1½ tablespoons all-purpose flour**
**¾ cup milk**
**2 tablespoons sliced pimiento-stuffed green olives**
**2 hard-cooked eggs, chopped**
**½ teaspoon salt**
**Dash pepper**
**1 tablespoon butter or margarine, melted**
**⅓ cup fine dry bread crumbs**

Cut squash in half; remove seeds. Bake, cut side down, in shallow pan at 350° for 35 to 45 minutes. Cook ham, green pepper, and celery in 2 tablespoons butter till tender.

Blend in flour; add milk all at once. Cook, stirring constantly, until mixture thickens and bubbles. Add olives, hard-cooked eggs, salt, and pepper. Spoon mixture into cavities of squash. Combine 1 tablespoon butter and bread crumbs; sprinkle over top. Bake at 350° for 15 minutes more. Makes 4 servings.

## Squash Chips

**Acorn squash**
**Salt**
**Ground ginger**

Peel and seed squash. Slice tissue paper-thin as for potato chips. Soak in ice water for 1 hour. Drain and pat dry. Fry in deep, hot fat (360°) until brown. Drain on paper toweling; sprinkle squash with salt and ginger.

## Delicata Bake

Quarter 2 delicata squash; seed. Bake in shallow pan at 350° till almost tender, about 40 minutes. Form 1 pound bulk pork sausage into 24 balls; brown in skillet. Drain.

Mix one 17-ounce can applesauce and 1 teaspoon ground cinnamon. Season squash with salt and pepper. Top squash with applesauce, then sausage. Bake 20 minutes more. Serves 8.

## Squash Soufflé

*Careful timing from oven to table is important—*

**3 pounds hubbard squash**
**1 cup milk**
**2 tablespoons butter or margarine**
**1 cup coarsely crushed, rich, round crackers (about 20 crackers)**
**2 tablespoons finely chopped, canned pimiento**
**1 teaspoon salt**
**1 teaspoon grated onion**
**Dash pepper**
**Dash ground nutmeg**
**2 well-beaten eggs**

Cut unpeeled squash into 3- to 4-inch squares. In a saucepan cook the squash, uncovered, in a small amount of boiling, salted water till tender, about 20 to 25 minutes. Remove pulp and mash (about 2 cups); discard rind.

In large saucepan heat together milk and butter over low heat till butter melts. Add *¾ cup* of the cracker crumbs; mix well. Add squash, pimiento, salt, onion, pepper, and nutmeg. Stir in eggs. Pour into 1-quart casserole; top with remaining ¼ cup crumbs. Bake at 350° till knife inserted just off-center comes out clean, about 1 hour. Garnish with additional pimiento strips, if desired. Serves 4 to 6.

## Golden Squash Soup

*Gives an autumn meal a different twist—*

**¼ cup chopped onion**
**2 tablespoons butter or margarine**
**2 tablespoons all-purpose flour**
**½ teaspoon salt**
**Dash pepper**
**Dash ground nutmeg**
**2 cups milk**
**1 cup chicken broth**
**1 cup cooked, mashed winter squash**
**2 tablespoons snipped parsley**

Cook onion in butter till tender but not brown. Blend in flour, salt, pepper, and nutmeg. Stir in remaining ingredients; cook and stir till mixture comes to boiling. Serve at once; garnish with parsley sprigs and a sprinkle of nutmeg, if desired. Serves 3 or 4.

**SQUAW CORN**—**1.** One of the five major types of corn, also known as flour corn. **2.** The name given to a dish containing corn and sometimes eggs and meat.

Squaw corn is native to the Western Hemisphere. Because it is made up mainly of soft starch, which is easier to chew and to grind, the Indians preferred it to dent, flint, sweet, and popcorn. These same Indians, who often depended on corn for their survival, later showed the early settlers how to grow, grind, and cook corn. That the early Americans took advantage of this instruction is seen in the many recipes using corn and cornmeal that have an Indian origin. Squaw Corn is a modern version.

## Squaw Corn

**1 12-ounce can luncheon meat**
**2 tablespoons chopped onion**
**1 16-ounce can cream-style corn**
**3 beaten eggs**

Dice or cut luncheon meat into thin strips. In skillet brown meat and onion. Add cream-style corn; heat till mixture is bubbly. Stir in the beaten eggs. Cook over low heat, stirring occasionally, just till eggs are set. Serve immediately sprinkled with snipped chives or parsley, if desired. Makes 6 servings.

**SQUID**—A marine animal that is related to the octopus and cuttlefish. The slender squid has 10 tentacles or arms attached to its head, and it can range in size from four inches to 80 feet. The coloring varies from white to red or brown.

These gourmet animals, with a sweet, rich meat, can be bought fresh, canned, or dried in specialty food stores. They are cooked and served in much the same way as are shellfish. The fresh meat will have a sweet smell when purchased and should be used within a day or two.

Squid meat contains protein, minerals, and the B vitamins. There are 85 calories in a 3½-ounce serving before cooking.

Stew squid in the liquid from its ink sac. You'll be surprised at the delightful flavor. If you wish, bake or sauté the squid whole, with or without a stuffing. Also use the tentacles. First chop up the squid, then dip it in a batter, and deep-fat fry it.

## Fried Squid

**2 pounds fresh or frozen squid**
• • •
**1 slightly beaten egg**
**¼ cup milk**
**⅔ cup fine saltine cracker crumbs**
**½ teaspoon salt**
**¼ teaspoon pepper**
**¼ cup shortening**

Thaw frozen squid. Clean and cut off head. Skin body portion, removing fins. Slit hollow body cavity; flatten and scrape clean with knife. Rinse well; pat dry. Combine egg and milk. Mix the fine cracker crumbs, salt, and pepper. Dip squid into egg mixture; then coat with crumbs. Heat shortening in heavy skillet. Add squid and cook quickly till done, about 2 minutes per side. Makes 6 servings.

**SQUIRREL**—A rodent that is taken for game. After dressing, the squirrel is cut up, then cooked much the same as chicken or rabbit. Before frying, cook

Keep a can of convenient luncheon meat and cream-style corn on hand to make this quick and easy Squaw Corn on those busy days.

squirrel for 30 minutes in a covered skillet with a small amount of liquid. This develops tenderness. (See also *Game*.)

## Fried Squirrel

Coat one 1- to 1½-pound ready-to-cook young squirrel, cut up, with mixture of ¼ cup all-purpose flour, ¾ teaspoon salt, and dash pepper. In skillet brown meat slowly in 2 tablespoons hot shortening. Reduce heat; add 2 or 3 tablespoons water. Cover; simmer till tender, about 30 minutes, adding more water if necessary. Makes 2 servings.

**STAINLESS STEEL**—A family of corrosion-resistant alloy steels used in manufacturing utensils, tableware, and household equipment. A minimum of 11 percent chromium is included in the alloys, with nickel or molybdenum added as needed to produce specific characteristics. Very durable, stainless steels do not pit, chip, or react to extreme temperature changes. In cookware, stainless steel is usually bonded to a copper, carbon steel, or aluminum core to improve heat distribution properties. (See also *Pots and Pans*.)

**STALE**—The quality of food that has lost its freshness but hasn't spoiled or become moldy. Usually associated with baked foods and cereal products, staling is a natural process that starts almost as soon as the food is out of the oven. However, you can retard staling by storing food properly and by using food wraps and reclosing packages, jars, and cans.

Temperature is an important factor, too. Refrigerator temperatures speed up staling, while freezer temperatures slow it down. From a staleness standpoint, it is better to store bread at room temperature or to freeze it than to refrigerate it. Fortunately, reheating the food or cereal in the oven revives much of the freshness.

**STAR ANISE**—The licorice-flavored seed of an herb with eight cloves, which form a star. Native to China, star anise has not been available in the United States for some years. (See also *Anise*.)

**STAYMAN APPLE**—A bright, red-skinned apple variety with an oval shape. Stayman's winelike flavor and all-purpose traits are indicative of its similarity to a Winesap apple. (See also *Apple*.)

**STARCH**—The edible carbohydrate of many types of plants, especially vegetables such as potatoes, corn, and legumes and cereal grains. In its pure form, starch is colorless, odorless, and tasteless. The size and shape of starch cells differ from one kind of plant to another. Nutritionally, starch provides energy for activity and to maintain vitality. In cooking, starch products such as flour, arrowroot, and cornstarch are used as thickening agents in gravies and puddings or to give structure to baked foods.

Because the body is able to use it so efficiently, starch is an important low-cost source of energy. An adequate supply of starch and other carbohydrates in the diet ensures that protein will be used for body-building and maintenance, not energy. However, once energy requirements are met, calories from an excess of starchy foods are stored in the body as fat.

**STEAK**—**1.** A crosscut slice of beef from the meaty part of the carcass. The word steak usually refers to one of the cuts from the rib, loin, sirloin, or round sections of the beef animal—those cuts that are tender enough for broiling and can be served rare, medium, or well-done. It can also refer to beefsteaks cut from the chuck or round that are usually specifically identified, such as blade steak.

**2.** A similar crosscut meaty slice that comes from another animal such as pork, veal, or game. The steaks from these animals are most commonly referred to as chops. **3.** A crosscut slice from a fish, particularly halibut, salmon, or swordfish. **4.** Ground beef or hamburger that is

***Juicy doneness***

Sizzle a juicy steak under the broiler while brushing with an onion-butter mixture to make Onion-Buttered Sirloin. →

shaped into a large patty called hamburger steak and cooked by broiling or panfrying. **5.** A slender, flat piece of beef, from the flank, which is a single muscle frequently marketed as flank steak.

***Nutritional value:*** Steaks from all meat animals as well as from fish, are excellent sources of high-quality protein. Vitamins and minerals are present in substantial quantities, too, but amounts vary somewhat among the species.

***How to buy:*** Since tenderness is the key word when selecting a steak, it is especially helpful to know what characteristics to look for at the meat counter. Bone shape (see *Meat* for Bone Shape Charts), government grade, and the amount of marbling are good indicators.

Tender steaks come from the rib, loin, and sirloin sections of the carcass. Each can be quickly identified by the shape of its bone. In the rib it is long and curved; in the loin it is the familiar T-bone; and the identifying bone in the sirloin is wedge-, round-, or oval-shaped.

As with most food rules, however, looking for the bone shape doesn't always apply. Some steaks are boneless. When this is the case, refer to the chart, or when in doubt, ask the meatman if the steak is from one of these three tender sections.

Slash through the fat layer just to the meat at one-inch intervals before broiling. This prevents curling of the meat during cooking.

Broilable steaks should be selected from U.S. Good, Choice, or Prime grades. Although the grade is stamped on the meat, always check the marbling – the fat that is streaked through the meat. Meat that is graded "Good" has the least and "Prime" the most, with "Choice" in between. Marbling contributes juiciness and flavor to a steak and keeps it from drying out during broiling. If the steak doesn't meet these criteria, braise it.

***How to cook:*** Depending on the tenderness of the cut, steaks are cooked by dry heat – panfrying, panbroiling, or broiling – if tender, and by moist heat if braising is needed to ensure tenderness.

Tender steaks cut less than one inch thick are usually cooked in a skillet or on a griddle rather than in a broiler oven or on a barbecue grill. If the meat is quite lean and if extra fat is added to the skillet, the method is called panfrying. If no additional fat is needed and if drippings are poured off as they accumulate, the method is called panbroiling. Broiling itself refers to cooking cuts at least one inch thick by direct heat in the broiler or by grilling on the barbecue.

In any case, first slash the fat just short of the lean, at one-inch intervals. This prevents the meat from curling. Then, cook to desired doneness. You can check doneness by making a small slit in the meat and observing the color: red is rare; pink is medium; and gray is well-done. After turning, season the steak and serve as is or with a favorite steak sauce.

Hamburger, although taken from less-tender cuts, is tender because it has been ground. The flank, when of high quality, can be considered a broilable steak, too. The other beefsteaks come from the round (identified by a round bone), and the chuck (identified by the blade bone, except for the arm steak, which has a round bone). Chuck and round steaks are usually braised to ensure tender eating. This is true of even Prime beef, although many people consider the chuck steaks that are cut next to the rib section satisfactory when broiled. Commercial tenderizers can be used to improve the broilability of these cuts.

| *Where Steaks Come From* | | |
|---|---|---|
| Location | | Name |
| Rib | Bone-in: | Rib Steak |
| | Boneless: | Rib Eye Steak, Delmonico |
| Loin | Bone-in: | Club Steak (no tenderloin), T-Bone Steak (small tenderloin), Porterhouse (large tenderloin) |
| | Boneless: | Strip Steak (tenderloin removed), also known as New York Cut or Kansas City Steak |
| | | Tenderloin also cut into Filet Mignon, Châteaubriand, and Tournedo |
| Sirloin | Bone-in: | Sirloin Steak |
| | Boneless: | Sirloin Steak—Top Sirloin and Sirloin (Butt) Steak |

## Stroganoff Steak Sandwich

Combine ⅔ cup beer, ⅓ cup salad oil, 1 teaspoon salt, ¼ teaspoon garlic powder, and ¼ teaspoon pepper. Place 1 flank steak (2 pounds) in mixture; cover. Marinate the steak overnight in refrigerator; drain.

Broil steak 3 inches from heat for 5 to 7 minutes on each side for medium-rare.

In saucepan melt 2 tablespoons butter or margarine. Blend in ½ teaspoon paprika and dash salt. Add 4 cups sliced onion. Cook till onion is tender but not brown.

To serve, slice meat on the diagonal across the grain of the meat. For each serving, arrange meat slices over 2 slices toasted French bread. Top with cooked onions. Combine 1 cup dairy sour cream, warmed, and ½ teaspoon prepared horseradish. Spoon mixture onto sandwiches. Sprinkle with paprika. Makes 6 servings.

## Mexican-Style Steak

**2 pounds round steak, ½ inch thick**
**3 tablespoons all-purpose flour**
**1½ teaspoons salt**
**Dash pepper**
**2 tablespoons salad oil**
• • •
**Salsa (Sauce)**
**1 6-ounce can broiled mushroom crowns, drained and halved**

Cut steak into 6 serving-sized pieces. Combine flour, salt, and pepper; dredge meat in mixture. Brown meat in hot salad oil; transfer to shallow baking dish. Pour half the Salsa (Sauce) over meat. Cover; bake at 325° till tender, about 2 hours. Add mushrooms the last 10 minutes. Skim off excess fat. Heat remaining Salsa; pass. Makes 6 servings.

*Salsa (Sauce):* Heat ¼ cup salad oil until hot. Add 1 clove garlic, crushed, and 1 cup chopped onion, stirring while mixture cooks. When onion and garlic are nicely browned, add one 28-ounce can tomatoes, mashed; one 4-ounce can chopped green chilies; and 1 teaspoon salt. Simmer the mixture, uncovered, about 30 minutes, stirring often. Salt to taste. Makes about 3 cups sauce.

## Onion-Buttered Sirloin

**½ cup butter or margarine**
**¼ cup snipped parsley**
**¼ cup minced onion**
**2 teaspoons Worcestershire sauce**
**½ teaspoon dry mustard**
**½ teaspoon freshly ground pepper**
**1 4-pound bone-in sirloin steak (about 1½ inches thick)**

In small saucepan combine butter or margarine, snipped parsley, minced onion, Worcestershire sauce, dry mustard, and freshly ground pepper. Heat together till butter melts.

Slash fat edges of sirloin steak at 1-inch intervals to prevent steak from curling. Place on rack in broiler pan. Broil 3 to 4 inches from heat for 7 to 8 minutes each side for rare or 10 to 12 minutes each side for medium, brushing with butter mixture. Place on platter; spoon remaining mixture over. Serves 8.

## Italian Steak

**1½ to 2 pounds beef blade steak, cut ¾ inch thick**
**2 tablespoons salad oil**
**1 3-ounce can sliced mushrooms, drained**
**½ cup chopped onion**
**2 tablespoons chopped green pepper**
**½ cup chili sauce**
**½ teaspoon salt**
**⅛ teaspoon pepper**
**¼ teaspoon dried oregano leaves, crushed**
**¼ teaspoon dry mustard**
**⅛ teaspoon garlic salt**
**½ teaspoon Worcestershire sauce**
**2 tablespoons sliced, pimiento-stuffed green olives**

Brown meat in a skillet in hot oil. Remove to an 8x8x2-inch baking dish. In the same skillet cook mushrooms, onion, and green pepper in oil till tender. Blend in remaining ingredients. Spoon over meat. Cover tightly and bake at 350° till tender, about 90 minutes. Remove meat to platter. Skim excess fat from sauce and pass sauce. Makes 6 servings.

## Ranch Round Steak

Trim excess fat from 3 pounds beef round steak, cut ½ inch thick. Cut meat into serving-sized pieces; slash edges. Combine ¼ cup all-purpose flour, 2 teaspoons dry mustard, 1½ teaspoons salt, and ⅛ teaspoon pepper; use to coat meat. Reserve remainder.

In skillet brown meat in hot oil. Push meat to one side. Stir in reserved flour mixture. Blend in ½ cup water and 1 tablespoon Worcestershire sauce. Cook and stir till thick; reduce heat. Simmer meat in gravy, covered, till tender, about 1¼ hours. Skim excess fat from gravy. Makes 8 servings.

## *Elegant steak entrée*

← Garnish spectacular Steak Diane with cooked, fluted mushrooms after preparing thin steak strips in chafing dish at the table.

Veal steaks are cut from the leg, loin, and shoulder portions. Although from a young animal, they lack fat and need moist cooking, or breading and frying or braising to make them tender and moist.

Lamb steaks are cut from the leg, loin, and shoulder, also. The latter two are usually called chops. Cook leg and loin steaks by broiling or panbroiling. Shoulder steaks are frequently braised.

Fresh pork steaks are shoulder and loin cuts with loin cuts sold as chops. Braise, broil, or panfry them slowly until well cooked. Ham steaks are cut from a cured and smoked pork leg. Many are purchased fully cooked. Panfry or broil these.

Broil, poach, or bake fish steaks in a sauce. Keep the surface moist and cook just till meat flakes.

**STEAK AU POIVRE** ***(stāk ō powv' ruh)***—Steak coated with cracked black peppercorns, then sautéed and served in sauce. *Poivre* is the French word for pepper.

**STEAK DIANE**—Tender steak, pounded thin, seasoned with dry mustard and black pepper, then cooked at the table in a chafing dish. A favorite of fine restaurants, it is easily duplicated at home.

## Steak Diane

**4 beef sirloin strip steaks, cut ½ inch thick**
**1 teaspoon dry mustard**
**¼ cup butter or margarine**
**3 tablespoons lemon juice**
**2 teaspoons snipped chives**
**1 teaspoon Worcestershire sauce**

Pound steaks to ⅓-inch thickness. Sprinkle one side with salt, freshly ground black pepper, and ⅛ *teaspoon* of the dry mustard; pound into meat. Repeat on other side. Heat blazer pan of chafing dish or skillet over direct flame. Then add butter; melt. Add 2 steaks and cook 2 minutes on each side. Transfer meat to hot serving plate. Repeat with remaining meat. To blazer pan add lemon juice, chives, and Worcestershire sauce; bring to boiling. Return meat to chafing dish. Spoon sauce over meat. Makes 4 servings.

**STEAK TARTARE** ***(tär' tuhr)***—A raw, chopped lean steak or scraped beef mixed with onion, garlic, other seasonings, and sometimes a raw egg yolk or whole egg.

Once, raw meat was consumed in large quantities, especially in the twelfth century by the followers of Genghis Khan, who considered it a quick source of strength. Today, however, cooks are aware of the possibilities of food poisoning, so they make sure that dishes such as steak tartare are handled carefully, kept refrigerated, and served promptly.

**STEAM**—To cook food with water vapor. Food is placed on a rack above the level of the water in a kettle that is covered tightly. Then, the water is brought to a boil. The resulting steam cooks the food. Another way to cook the food is in a special utensil called a steamer, which is built like a double boiler with perforations in the bottom of the top pan. This allows the steam to rise through the food. Steamers come in sizes small enough to cook a serving of vegetables or large enough to steam a peck of clams.

Vegetables that are panned in a tightly covered skillet are also steamed. The steam is formed from their own juices and from the liquid in the cooking fat.

**STEEP**—To extract color, flavor, or other qualities from a food by letting it stand in water that is just below the boiling point. Tea, for example, is steeped to extract flavor and color from the leaves.

**STEINWEIN**—A greenish gold wine produced in Würzburg, Germany. Made from Sylvaner and Riesling grapes, *Steinwein* is bottled in a stocky flask called a *Bocksbeutel.* The wine is characteristically dry with fuller body and better keeping qualities than either Rhine or Moselle wines. Some wines produced in close proximity to Würzburg are also marketed in *Bocksbeutel* and are incorrectly named *Steinwein.*

**STERILIZE** ***(ster' uh līz')***—To destroy disease- and spoilage-producing microorganisms by applying heat. To keep a food sterile after having exposed it to air, you must use it immediately or seal it in an airtight container (such as is done in canning foods). Otherwise, microorganisms are quickly reintroduced.

**STEW**—**1.** To simmer food slowly in liquid. **2.** A food mixture, usually a combination of meat and vegetables, that is cooked by slowly simmering it in a liquid.

Although ingredients and preparation techniques differ from country to country, stew is a universal dish. In the United States, stews—most frequently named for their main ingredient—are usually thickened with flour, while stews in Czechoslovakia often are thickened with pumpernickel crumbs. In Argentina a sweet potato sauce is the thickening agent.

Most countries have their own names for stew. For example, in France stews are called *ragout* or *carbonnade;* in Italy, fish stew is called *cioppino,* while *stufato* refers to a beef stew. The equivalent of stew in India is called a curry and in Japan stew is known as sukiyaki.

Actually, it's much more of a cooking art to make a perfect stew than it is to broil a perfect steak. The most important part of making a good stew is long, slow cooking. Allow plenty of time for the meat to become tender, then add the vegetables just long enough before the stew is done to let them cook properly without overcooking (that is time enough for the vegetables to contribute their flavor without losing their bright colors).

## Lobster and Corn Stew

**2 tablespoons butter or margarine**
**1/4 cup chopped onion**
**2 tablespoons chopped green pepper**
**1 17-ounce can whole kernel corn, undrained**
**1 5-ounce can lobster, drained and flaked**
**1 cup light cream**
**1 cup milk**

Melt butter in 2-quart saucepan. Add onion and green pepper; cook till tender. Add remaining ingredients, 1/2 teaspoon salt, and dash white pepper. Heat through. Serves 4 or 5.

## Irish Lamb Stew

Trim fat from 2 or 3 lean lamb shoulder chops (at least 1 pound total). Cut meat into 1- to 1½-inch squares. Barely cover meat and bones with water (about 1¼ cups).

Cover pan; simmer (don't boil) 45 minutes. Add 1 medium potato, quartered; 2 or 3 small carrots, cut in thirds; 1 medium onion, quartered; one ½-inch slice peeled medium rutabaga, diced (optional); 1 large celery stalk, cut in ½-inch lengths, plus a few leaves; 1 small green pepper, cut in ½-inch strips; 1¼ teaspoons salt; and dash white pepper. Cover and simmer till meat and vegetables are tender, about 20 to 30 minutes. Remove bones.

Put 3 tablespoons water in shaker; add 1½ tablespoons flour and shake till smooth. Remove stew from heat; stir flour mixture into stew. Return to heat. Cook and stir till thickened. Add 2 tablespoons snipped parsley. Salt to taste. Makes 4 servings.

## Beef Stew with Biscuit Topper

**2 pounds beef chuck, cut in 1-inch cubes**
**¼ cup all-purpose flour**
**¼ teaspoon dry mustard**
**⅛ teaspoon paprika**
**3 tablespoons shortening**
**2 beef bouillon cubes**
**¾ cup chopped onion**

• • •

**1 10-ounce package frozen peas and carrots, thawed**
**¼ cup snipped parsley**
**Buttermilk Biscuits *or* 1 8-ounce tube buttermilk biscuits**

Coat meat generously with a mixture of flour, mustard, paprika, 1½ teaspoons salt, and ⅛ teaspoon pepper. Brown meat well in hot shortening. Dissolve bouillon in 2½ cups boiling water. Combine beef, bouillon, and onion in 2-quart casserole or oven-going skillet. Cover and bake at 375° for 1¼ hours. Stir in vegetables and parsley. Bake 15 minutes longer. Remove from oven. Increase oven temperature to 450°. Place Buttermilk Biscuits, overlapping, around edge of dish, atop *hot* meat mixture. Bake, uncovered, till biscuits are golden and vegetables are cooked. Serves 6 to 8.

*Buttermilk Biscuits:* Sift together 1 cup sifted all-purpose flour, 1½ teaspoons baking powder, ¼ teaspoon salt, and ⅛ teaspoon baking soda. Cut in 3 tablespoons shortening till mixture resembles coarse crumbs. Make well in center; add ⅓ cup buttermilk all at once. Stir quickly with fork till dough follows fork around bowl. Turn onto lightly floured surface (dough should be soft). Knead gently 10 to 12 strokes. Roll or pat dough ⅛ inch thick. Dip cutter in flour; cut dough straight down—no twisting. Cut each biscuit in half.

## Scottish Lamb Stew

**2 pounds lean lamb, cut in 1-inch cubes**
**2 tablespoons salad oil**
**1 10¾-ounce can condensed Scotch broth**
**1 medium onion, cut in wedges**
**¼ cup water**
**1 clove garlic, minced**
**½ teaspoon dried thyme leaves, crushed**
**1 2½-ounce package sour cream sauce mix**

In medium skillet brown half the lamb at a time in hot oil. Add Scotch broth, onion wedges, water, garlic, and thyme. Cover and simmer till meat is tender, 50 to 60 minutes. Prepare sour cream sauce mix according to package directions; stir into lamb mixture. Cook over low heat just till hot. Serves 6.

## Beef Stew Bake

*An easy oven meal—*

In heavy skillet brown 1½ pounds beef stew meat, cut in 1½-inch cubes, in 2 tablespoons hot shortening; drain off excess fat. Add one 10½-ounce can mushroom gravy, 1 cup tomato juice, ½ envelope dry onion soup mix (¼ cup), and 1 teaspoon prepared horseradish. Simmer, covered, for 5 minutes. Place 4 medium potatoes, peeled and quartered, in bottom of a 2-quart casserole. Top with meat mixture. Bake, covered, at 350° till meat and potatoes are tender, about 1½ hours, stirring once or twice during baking. Makes 6 servings.

Plan on serving second helpings of Beef Stew with Biscuit Topper. This updated version of an old favorite combines processed foods—frozen vegetables—with traditional ingredients.

## Chinese Stew

Sprinkle 2 pounds beef stew meat, cut in 1-inch cubes, with 1/8 teaspoon pepper. Brown in 1 tablespoon salad oil. Add one 10½-ounce can condensed golden mushroom soup; 1¼ cups water; 1 small onion, thinly sliced; and 2 tablespoons soy sauce. Cover and simmer till tender, 1½ hours. Add 1 small head cabbage *or* Chinese cabbage, cut in 1-inch pieces, and one 5-ounce can bamboo shoots, drained. Cover; simmer 8 minutes. Serves 6.

## Tomato Chili Stew

**1 11½-ounce can condensed bean with bacon soup**
**1 10¾-ounce can condensed tomato soup**
**1 10½-ounce can chili con carne without beans**
**1 soup can water**

In saucepan combine all ingredients. Simmer 10 minutes. Makes 5 or 6 servings.

## Beef Ball Oven Stew

**1 beaten egg**
**½ cup milk**
**¼ cup yellow cornmeal**
**2 tablespoons chopped green pepper**
**1 tablespoon instant minced onion**
**1 teaspoon dry mustard**
**½ to 1 teaspoon chili powder**
**1 pound ground beef**
**2 tablespoons all-purpose flour**
**2 tablespoons shortening**
**3 potatoes, peeled and quartered**
**3 medium onions, quartered**
**6 carrots, peeled and cut in thin strips 2 inches long**
**1 18-ounce can tomato juice**
**½ bay leaf, crushed**

Combine first 7 ingredients and ¾ teaspoon salt. Add meat; mix. Form into 12 balls.

Lightly coat meatballs in flour, reserving remaining flour. Brown in hot shortening. Place meatballs in 3-quart casserole, reserving pan juices. To casserole add potatoes, onions, and carrots. Season with salt and pepper.

Blend reserved flour (about 4 teaspoons) into reserved pan juices. Stir in tomato juice and bay leaf. Cook and stir till thickened and bubbly. Pour atop casserole. Cover; bake at 350° for 1 to 1¼ hours. Serves 6.

## Veal Stew with Ravioli

**3 tablespoons all-purpose flour**
**1 pound veal stew meat, cut in 1-inch cubes**
**4 teaspoons shortening**
**¼ cup chopped onion**
**1 small clove garlic, minced**
**1 10-ounce package frozen peas**
**1 16-ounce can ravioli**
**2 tablespoons snipped parsley**
**¼ teaspoon dried oregano leaves, crushed**

Combine flour, 1 teaspoon salt, and dash pepper. Coat meat with all the flour mixture. Brown in hot shortening. Add onion and garlic. Cook 4 to 5 minutes. Add 1½ cups water; cover and simmer till meat is tender, about 1 hour. Add remaining ingredients. Cook 15 minutes, stirring occasionally. Serves 4.

## Dilled Lamb Stew

**2 pounds boneless lamb, cut in ¾-inch cubes**
**2 tablespoons shortening**
**½ teaspoon dillweed**
**2 cups sliced carrot**
**1 cup sliced celery**
**2 tablespoons all-purpose flour**
**1 cup dairy sour cream**

Brown lamb in hot shortening. Season with mixture of 1 teaspoon salt and dillweed; add 2 cups water. Cover and simmer till meat is almost tender, 35 minutes. Add carrot and celery; cook 15 minutes. Blend flour and ¾ cup cold water; stir into stew. Cook till mixture thickens and bubbles. Stir in sour cream; heat through (do not boil). Serves 6.

## Vegetable-Meatball Stew

**1 beaten egg**
**¼ cup milk**
**¾ cup soft bread crumbs**
**2 tablespoons chopped green onion**
**1 teaspoon dry mustard**
**¼ teaspoon dried thyme leaves, crushed**
**1 pound ground beef**
**2 tablespoons shortening**
**1 beef bouillon cube**
**2 tablespoons all-purpose flour**
**¼ teaspoon Kitchen Bouquet**
**1 16-ounce can whole carrots**
**1 16-ounce can whole onions**
**1 3-ounce can sliced mushrooms**

Combine egg, milk, bread crumbs, green onion, dry mustard, thyme, ½ teaspoon salt, and dash pepper. Add meat; mix well. Shape into 24 balls. In skillet brown meatballs slowly in hot shortening, about 10 minutes, shaking the skillet to turn meatballs.

Meanwhile, dissolve bouillon cube in 1⅓ cups boiling water; set aside. Remove meatballs from skillet; skim fat from pan drippings. Blend flour into drippings. Add bouillon. Cook and stir till thickened and bubbly. Stir in Kitchen Bouquet; season with salt and pepper to taste. Drain carrots, onions, and mushrooms. Add vegetables and meatballs to skillet; cover and heat through. Makes 6 servings.

## Good Neighbor Stew

**1 pound beef stew meat, cut in 1-inch cubes**
**1 tablespoon salad oil**
**1 cup chopped onion**
**1 clove garlic, minced**
**1 16-ounce can tomatoes, cut up**
**½ teaspoon sugar**
**3 large carrots, sliced ½ inch thick (1½ cups)**
**1 10-ounce package frozen, small onions in cream sauce**
**1 3-ounce can sliced mushrooms, drained (½ cup)**

Brown meat in hot oil. Add onion and garlic and cook till onion is tender. Stir in tomatoes, 1 teaspoon salt, sugar, and dash pepper. Cook, covered, for 45 minutes over low heat, stirring occasionally. Add sliced carrots and cook 30 minutes more. Add frozen onions in cream sauce and the mushrooms. Cook till meat is tender, about 15 minutes. Makes 4 servings.

## Veal Stew 'n Dumplings

**1½ pounds veal, cut in 1-inch cubes**
**All-purpose flour**
**Shortening**
**4 cups tomato juice**
**4 to 6 drops bottled hot pepper sauce**
**1 cup diced, peeled potatoes**
**½ cup sliced celery**
**½ cup chopped onion**
**Cornmeal Dumplings**

Coat veal with flour. Brown slowly in small amount of hot shortening in Dutch oven. Add tomato juice, 2 teaspoons salt, and bottled hot pepper sauce. Cover; simmer 1 hour.

Add potatoes, celery, and chopped onion; cover and cook till vegetables are almost tender, about 30 minutes. Drop Cornmeal Dumplings by rounded tablespoons onto *hot, bubbling* stew. Cover tightly; steam 10 minutes (don't lift cover). Makes 6 servings.

*Cornmeal Dumplings:* Combine one 10-ounce package corn bread mix and 2 tablespoons snipped parsley. Then, prepare mix according to package directions, *except* use ⅓ cup milk.

**STICK CINNAMON**—The name for long, slender pieces of whole cinnamon or rolled cinnamon bark. (See also *Cinnamon.*)

## Spiced Fruit Sparkle

**⅔ cup sugar**
**1½ cups water**
**6 inches stick cinnamon**
**12 whole cloves**
**1 6-ounce can frozen pineapple juice concentrate**
**1 6-ounce can frozen orange juice concentrate**
**2 cups water**
**¼ cup lemon juice**

• • •

**Ice cubes**
**1 28-ounce bottle ginger ale, chilled**
**Cinnamon sticks**

In medium saucepan combine sugar, 1½ cups water, 6 inches stick cinnamon, and whole cloves. Simmer, covered, 15 minutes; strain. Cool. Put juice concentrates, 2 cups water, and lemon juice in blender container; blend till frothy. Add to strained mixture; chill.

Before serving, pour mixture over ice cubes in punch bowl. Slowly pour chilled ginger ale into bowl. Serve along with cinnamon stick stirrers. Makes about 2 quarts.

## Frosty Spiced Tea

**¾ cup water**
**¼ cup sugar**
**½ teaspoon whole cloves**
**6 inches stick cinnamon, broken**
**¼ teaspoon ground nutmeg**
**1 quart boiling water**

• • •

**6 teaspoons loose tea *or* 6 tea bags**
**Ice cubes**

In saucepan combine ¾ cup water, sugar, cloves, cinnamon, and nutmeg; cover and simmer for 20 minutes. Strain to remove spices. Pour the boiling water over tea and steep for 4 minutes; strain. Add spiced syrup and pour over ice cubes in glasses. Makes 6 servings.

## Daiquiri Blazer

In blazer pan of chafing dish combine 1½ cups hot water, ¼ cup sugar, 6 inches stick cinnamon, and 8 whole cloves. Bring to boiling over direct heat; cook 5 minutes. Add one 6-ounce can frozen lemonade concentrate, thawed, and one 6-ounce can frozen limeade concentrate, thawed; return mixture to boiling.

In small saucepan heat ⅔ cup light rum; ignite. Pour over hot beverage. Ladle into demitasse cups. Makes 8 to 10 servings.

**STILL WINE**—A nonsparkling wine. Any young wine that has fermented completely or older wine that contains no effervescence can be called a still wine.

**STILTON CHEESE** ***(stil' tuhn)***—A blue-veined cheese that is made of rich milk and additional cream. Stilton is named for a parish in Huntingdonshire, England.

This semisoft, rather spicy cheese is delicious served as a snack or with fruit for dessert. (See also *Cheese*.)

**STINGER** ***(sting' uhr)***—An after-dinner cocktail of brandy and creme de menthe.

## Stinger

**1 jigger brandy (1½ ounces)**
**1 jigger white crème de menthe (1½ ounces)**
**½ cup crushed or cracked ice**

Place brandy, white crème de menthe, and ice in blender container. Blend ingredients quickly. Strain into glass. Makes 1.

**STIR**—To agitate a mixture by moving a spoon or other utensil through it in a circular motion. Stirring is used both to blend ingredients and to keep a mixture from sticking to the pan while cooking.

**STIR FRY**—A Chinese cooking technique that involves quick cooking and constant stirring. Cut-up vegetables are the foods most commonly stir fried. This technique enables the cook to stop the cooking while the vegetables are still crisp-tender. (See also *Oriental Cookery*.)

**STIRRED CUSTARD**—A mixture of eggs, milk, and sugar that is thickened by heating on top of the range, often in a double

To prevent lumps in Stirred Custard, add some of the hot milk to the egg mixture, then stir this mixture into rest of milk.

Stirred Custard is done when it coats a metal spoon. At this stage, remove it from the heat and cool in a cold water bath.

***Uses for stirred custard***

Serve chilled Stirred Custard as a sauce over baked chocolate soufflé, apple dumplings, chilled poached pears or other fruit, baked fruit puddings, and other desserts.

boiler, until the eggs coagulate. To prevent the custard from sticking to the pan, you must stir it constantly; hence, the name stirred custard. (See also *Custard*.)

### Snow Pudding with Berries

**1/3 cup sugar**
**1/8 teaspoon salt**
**2 teaspoons unflavored gelatin**
**1/4 teaspoon grated lemon peel**
**2 tablespoons lemon juice**

• • •

**2 unbeaten egg whites**
**Custard Sauce**
**Fresh strawberries, cut in halves**

In saucepan combine sugar, salt, and unflavored gelatin. Add 1/3 cup cold water. Stir over low heat to dissolve. Remove from heat; add 1/4 cup cold water, lemon peel, and lemon juice. Chill till partially set.

Turn into bowl; add unbeaten egg whites. Beat with electric or rotary beater till mixture begins to hold its shape. Pour into five 5-ounce custard cups. Chill till firm. To serve, unmold. Drizzle with Custard Sauce. Top with strawberry halves. Serves 5.

*Custard Sauce:* In heavy saucepan combine 3/4 cup skim milk, 2 beaten egg yolks, 4 teaspoons sugar, and dash salt. Cook and stir over very low heat till mixture coats metal spoon. Remove from heat; cool immediately by placing pan in cold water. Stir several minutes; stir in 1/2 teaspoon vanilla. Chill.

### *A light meal ending*

← Spoon the smooth custard sauce over the gelatin mounds, then trim with strawberry halves for Snow Pudding with Berries.

### Stirred Custard

**3 slightly beaten eggs**
**1/4 cup sugar**
**1/4 teaspoon salt**
**2 cups milk, scalded**
**1/2 teaspoon vanilla**

Combine eggs, sugar, and salt. Slowly stir in slightly cooled milk. Cook in heavy saucepan over very low heat,* stirring constantly. As soon as custard coats metal spoon, remove from heat. Cool at once; place pan in cold water and stir a minute or two. Add vanilla. Chill thoroughly. Makes 5 or 6 servings.

*Or cook in double boiler, over *hot, not boiling* water, stirring constantly.

### Baked Prune Whip

**4 egg whites**
**1/4 teaspoon salt**
**1/4 teaspoon cream of tartar**
**1/4 cup sugar**

• • •

**1 1/2 cups cooked prunes, drained**
**1 1/2 teaspoons grated lemon peel**
**2 teaspoons lemon juice**
**Stirred Custard**

Beat egg whites, salt, and cream of tartar to soft peaks. Gradually add *3 tablespoons* of the sugar; beat to stiff peaks. Snip cooked prunes into small pieces; add remaining sugar, peel, and juice; beat well. Fold into whites. Bake in a greased 11 3/4x7 1/2x1 3/4-inch baking dish at 350° till knife comes out clean, about 30 minutes. Serve with sauce of Stirred Custard. Makes 6 to 8 servings.

**STOCK**—A flavorful broth made by slowly cooking meat, fish, and/or vegetables in seasoned water. There are two common types of meat stock—brown stock and white stock. Brown stock is made with beef; white stock, with veal or chicken.

Stock is used as the base for many kinds of soups and sauces, and it can be the liquid used in making a variety of gravies. Sometimes, stock is made even fuller flavored by cooking it down to a jellylike consistency before using it.

## Brown Stock

**6 pounds beef soup bones, cut in pieces**
**2½ quarts cold water**
**1 cup sliced onion**
**½ cup chopped celery**
**1 large bay leaf**
**4 sprigs parsley**
**8 whole black peppercorns**

Place meat bones and cold water in large kettle. Simmer, uncovered, (*don't boil*) 3 hours. Remove bones; cut off meat and chop. Return meat to stock; add remaining ingredients and 2 teaspoons salt. Simmer, uncovered, 2 hours longer. Strain. (Use meat in soup or hash.) Clarify stock, if desired. Skim off fat, *or* chill and lift off fat. Makes 6 cups.

*To clarify stock:* Crush 1 eggshell; mix with white of 1 egg and ¼ cup water. Stir into hot stock. Bring the mixture to boiling. Let stand 5 minutes; strain.

## White Stock

**1 3- to 4-pound veal knuckle, cut in several pieces**
**3 quarts cold water**
**2 stalks celery**
**1 onion, quartered**
**1 carrot, sliced**
**2 sprigs parsley**
**2 cloves garlic**
**½ bay leaf**
**8 whole black peppercorns**
**1 tablespoon salt**

In soup kettle combine veal knuckle, cold water, celery, onion, carrot, parsley, garlic, bay leaf, peppercorns, and salt.

Simmer, uncovered, (*don't boil*) 5 hours. Strain. Clarify, if desired (see recipe for Brown Stock). Use in cream soups for part or all of the milk. Makes about 2 quarts.

**STOLLEN** ***(stōl' uhn)***—A rich, German yeast sweet bread filled with fruits and nuts. The baked bread is topped with a glaze and/or additional fruits. In Germany, stollen is a traditional Christmas treat. (See also *German Cookery.*)

## German Stollen

*Subtly spiced with cardamom—*

**1 package active dry yeast**
**4 to 4½ cups sifted all-purpose flour**
**¼ teaspoon ground cardamom**
**1¼ cups milk**
**½ cup butter or margarine**
**¼ cup sugar**
**1 teaspoon salt**
**1 slightly beaten egg**

• • •

**1 cup seedless raisins**
**¼ cup currants**
**¼ cup chopped mixed candied fruits**
**2 tablespoons grated orange peel**
**1 tablespoon grated lemon peel**
**¼ cup chopped, blanched almonds**

• • •

**Glaze**

In large mixer bowl combine yeast, *2 cups* of the flour, and cardamom. Heat milk, butter or margarine, sugar, and salt just till warm, stirring occasionally to melt butter. Add to dry mixture in mixer bowl; add egg. Beat at low speed with electric mixer for ½ minute, scraping sides of bowl constantly. Beat 3 minutes at high speed. By hand, stir in fruits, peels, and nuts. Stir in enough of remaining flour to make a soft dough.

Turn out on a lightly floured surface. Knead till smooth and elastic, about 8 to 10 minutes. Place in a greased bowl, turning once to grease surface of dough. Cover and let rise in warm place till double, about 1¾ hours. Punch down; turn out on a lightly floured surface. Divide dough into 3 equal parts. Cover; let dough rest 10 minutes.

Roll each of the 3 parts into a 10x6-inch rectangle. Without stretching, fold the long side of each rectangle over to within 1 inch of the opposite side; seal edge. Place on greased baking sheets. Cover and let rise in a warm place till almost double, about 1 hour. Bake at 375° till golden brown, 15 to 20 minutes. While warm, brush with Glaze. To match picture, top Stollen with additional pieces of candied fruits. Makes 3 loaves.

*Glaze:* Combine 1 cup sifted confectioners' sugar, 2 tablespoons hot water, and ½ teaspoon butter or margarine. Brush over stollen.

Follow the German tradition and serve German Stollen glazed and decorated with candied fruits as a Christmas treat. Or bake it any time when the occasion demands a special bread.

**STOUT**—A very dark beer that has a strong malt and hop flavor as well as a mild, sweet taste. Much of the flavor and color of stout is due to the use of roasted malt. Both England and Ireland are famous for their stouts. (See also *Beer*.)

**STRAIN**—To filter, usually through a cloth or fine wire mesh. The technique of straining is commonly used to remove lumps from gravy, whole spices from beverages, and tea leaves from brewed tea.

**STRAINER**—A sieve used to separate solids from liquids. Common kitchen strainers range from tea strainers, which consist of a small cup of fine wire mesh attached to a handle, to colanders, which are bowl-like utensils with fairly large holes in them. (See also *Utensil*.)

**STRATA**—A casserole made up of several layers of food, usually including bread and sliced or shredded cheese, bound together with a sauce or egg mixture.

## Sausage Strata

6 slices white bread
1 pound bulk pork sausage
1 teaspoon prepared mustard
4 ounces process Swiss cheese, shredded (1 cup)
3 slightly beaten eggs
1¼ cups milk
¾ cup light cream
1 teaspoon Worcestershire sauce
½ teaspoon salt
Dash pepper
Dash ground nutmeg

Fit bread into bottom of greased 12x7½x2-inch baking dish. Brown sausage; *drain off all excess fat.* Stir in mustard. Spoon sausage evenly over bread; sprinkle with shredded cheese. Combine slightly beaten eggs, milk, cream, Worcestershire sauce, salt, pepper, and ground nutmeg; pour over cheese. Bake at 325° till set, about 30 minutes. Serves 6.

## Company Strata

12 slices white bread
12 ounces sharp process cheese, sliced
1 10-ounce package frozen, chopped broccoli, cooked and drained
2 cups diced fully cooked ham
6 slightly beaten eggs
3½ cups milk
2 tablespoons instant minced onion
¼ teaspoon dry mustard

From the bread, cut 12 "doughnuts and holes." Fit the scraps of bread (top crusts removed) in bottom of 13x9x2-inch baking dish. Layer sliced cheese, cooked broccoli, and diced ham over bread. Arrange "doughnuts and holes" atop. Combine eggs, milk, instant minced onion, ½ teaspoon salt, and mustard; pour over bread. Cover; refrigerate 6 hours. Bake, uncovered, at 325° for 55 minutes. *Let stand 10 minutes before cutting.* Makes 12 servings.

Entertain dinner guests without last-minute rush by making Company Strata the main dish. This ham-broccoli-cheese casserole is made ahead and refrigerated until time to bake.

## Chicken Strata

**6 slices day-old white bread**
**2 cups cubed, cooked chicken *or* turkey**
**½ cup chopped onion**
**½ cup finely chopped celery**
**¼ cup chopped green pepper**
**½ cup mayonnaise**
**¾ teaspoon salt**
**Dash pepper**

• • •

**2 slightly beaten eggs**
**1½ cups milk**
**1 10½-ounce can condensed cream of mushroom soup**
**½ cup shredded sharp process American cheese**

Butter 2 *slices* bread; cut in ½-inch cubes and set aside. Cut remaining bread in 1-inch cubes; place *half of unbuttered cubes* in bottom of 8x8x2-inch baking dish. Combine chicken, *or* turkey, onion, celery, green pepper, mayonnaise, salt, and pepper. Spoon over bread cubes. Sprinkle remaining unbuttered cubes over chicken mixture. Combine eggs and milk; pour over all. Cover and chill 1 hour or overnight. Spoon soup over top. Sprinkle with buttered cubes. Bake at 325° till set, about 60 minutes. Sprinkle shredded cheese over top last few minutes of baking. Let stand a few minutes before serving. Makes 6 servings.

## Ham and Vegetable Strata

Combine one 10½-ounce can condensed cream of mushroom soup and 2 slightly beaten eggs; gradually stir in 1½ cups milk. Cut 4 slices day-old bread into 1-inch cubes; place *half* of the cubes in bottom of 9x9x2-inch baking dish. Top with 1½ cups finely diced fully cooked ham; spoon 1 cup cooked peas over ham. Sprinkle remaining bread cubes over ham-vegetable mixture; pour soup mixture over all. Cover and refrigerate 6 to 24 hours.

Spread 1 tablespoon butter or margarine on 2 slices day-old bread; cut in ½-inch cubes. Sprinkle casserole with buttered cubes. Bake at 325° till set, about 50 to 60 minutes. Sprinkle ½ cup shredded sharp process American cheese over top last few minutes of baking. Let stand 10 minutes before serving. Serves 6.

## Cheese-Corn Strata

**8 slices day-old bread**
**8 ounces sharp natural Cheddar cheese, sliced**
**1 16-ounce can whole kernel corn, undrained**
**4 beaten eggs**
**2½ cups milk**
**2 tablespoons minced onion**
**½ teaspoon prepared mustard**

Trim crusts from 5 *slices* of the bread; cut in half diagonally. Use trimmings and remaining 3 slices *untrimmed* bread to cover bottom of 9-inch square baking dish. Top with sliced cheese. Spread whole kernel corn over top of cheese layer. Arrange the 10 trimmed "triangles" in 2 rows atop corn. (Points should overlap bases of preceding "triangles.")

Combine beaten eggs, milk, onion, 1 teaspoon salt, mustard, and dash pepper. Pour over bread and corn. Cover with waxed paper; let stand 1 hour at room temperature or several hours in refrigerator. Bake at 325° till knife inserted halfway between center and edge comes out clean, about 1 hour. Let stand 5 minutes before serving. Makes 6 servings.

## Tuna-Cheese Strata

**6 slices white bread**
**1 6½- or 7-ounce can tuna, drained and flaked**
**¼ cup mayonnaise or salad dressing**
**1 tablespoon chopped pimiento**
**2 teaspoons instant minced onion**
**2 beaten eggs**
**1½ cups milk**
**1 10¾-ounce can condensed Cheddar cheese soup**

Cube *2 slices* of the bread and reserve; trim crusts from remaining 4 slices, if desired. Place the 4 slices bread in bottom of 8x8x2-inch baking dish. Combine tuna, mayonnaise, pimiento, and onion. Spread mixture over bread in pan. Sprinkle bread cubes atop tuna mixture. Combine eggs and milk; pour over all. Cover and chill at least 1 hour. Stir soup and spoon over top. Bake, uncovered, at 325° till set, about 1 hour. Remove from oven. Let stand 5 minutes before cutting. Serves 4.

# STRAWBERRY

***A collection of facts, figures, and irresistible recipes for these heart-shaped fruits.***

Alluring fragrance, brilliant red color, and sweet flavor are three outstanding reasons why strawberries are one of man's favorite fruits. At first available only in their small, sweet, wild form, strawberries were a luxury. Today, however, improved cultivation makes possible an ample supply of these large, succulent berries for all people to enjoy.

Through the centuries, strawberries have been given an assortment of names in many different languages. The English word for these delectable fruits seemingly evolved from the early Anglo-Saxon word *streowberie*, which was used to describe the strewed appearance of the plant stems and the spreading characteristic of the plant runners. Over the years, the spelling of this word changed several times, finally reaching its modern form in 1538.

As with the origin of the name, there are fairly accurate accounts of the development of strawberries from the wild to the cultivated form. Archaeological remains show that various types of wild strawberries have been growing on the European and American continents for centuries. The Roman writers Virgil and Pliny wrote about the wild strawberries that their civilization used. These berries were aromatic and tasty, but the yields were low and the size of the berries was small. Even cultivation of this wild form, which began in the 1400s, did not eliminate the shortcomings of the wild plants.

### *Strawberries upon strawberries*

← Dollops of whipped cream crown the plump, glistening berries in Strawberry Glaze Pie, always a welcome spring or summer dessert.

The evolution of strawberries into today's form was brought about by the crossing of two distinct wild strawberry varieties, one of which was indigenous to North America; the other, to South America. As North America was colonized, the settlers found an abundance of wild meadow strawberries that were sweeter in flavor than and outproduced any of the European types. These plants were taken first to France, then later to England and other European countries. Both the plants and the small-sized fruits thrived in these areas. Likewise, in 1712, Captain Frezier, a Frenchman, imported into France walnut-sized, yellow-colored strawberries that were grown by the Indians in Chile. The chance crossing of the American meadow and the Chilean yellow (beach) strawberries resulted in plants that produced flavorful, strawberries similar to those eaten today.

Strawberry hybridization and cultivation on a commercial scale were natural outgrowths of these crossings. In 1838, horticulturist Charles Hovey introduced the improved Hovey strawberry variety. This was the first known artificial cross of any fruit in the United States. After 1860, cultivation of strawberries expanded quickly due to the availability of better varieties and transportation.

***How strawberries are produced:*** The structure of strawberry plants forms the basis for their cultivation. The production techniques used ensure a large yield per acre and the best quality fruit.

Strawberry plants grow close to the soil surface and develop into two main parts above the ground, runners and stalks. During the growing season, the plants send out shoots or runners that, in time, attach themselves to the ground and develop into new plants. From the plant stalks, both leaves and flowers develop.

Pollination of the flowers results in fruit formation. Some plants flower in the spring and bear only one crop of fruit in the summer. Others, commonly known as everbearers, continually flower and fruit until cold weather sets in.

For most commercial purposes, strawberry plants, although perennial, are retained for only one to four years, then are tilled under and replaced by new plants. Special spacing, soil cultivating, and mulching techniques are used to promote the best fruit yield and to make the picking operation as easy as possible.

Strawberries can grow under a variety of climatic and soil conditions. Because of the year-round growing seasons, California and Florida are the largest producing regions in the United States. Smaller commercial operations are located in most of the other states, too.

***Nutritional value:*** If you're calorie- and nutrition-conscious, fresh strawberries fit right into your needs. They are low in calories and add important vitamins and minerals to the diet, too. One cup of unsweetened fresh strawberries contains 55 calories. Although citrus fruits are most commonly associated with vitamin C, fresh strawberries are equally good contributors of this important nutrient. Small amounts of many other vitamins and minerals are also present in strawberries.

***Types of strawberries:*** The varietal names of strawberries are of greater importance to growers than they are to homemakers. Growers select strawberry varieties to raise after considering several factors – where they are to be grown, when and how often the berries ripen, and what form (fresh, frozen, or canned) in which they will be sold. Although the list of varieties fills a thick book, about 15 varieties account for 90 percent of the berries that are commercially marketed.

Even with the extensive hybridization of strawberries that has and is being done, the flavor and fragrance of wild strawberries has never been duplicated. Take advantage of any chance that you may have to use these delicacies even though they may seem quite small in comparison to cultivated strawberries.

## How to select

Not long ago, fresh strawberries could be purchased only during summer months, but with the development of more versatile strawberry varieties, many markets in the United States can supply these fresh favorites practically all year. In general, the peak season for fresh strawberries (and when they are most economical) is between April and July. Sweetened and unsweetened frozen berries and canned strawberries packed in syrup, as pie fillings, or as jellies, jams, and preserves, expand the selection of strawberry products that can be selected year-round.

When selecting fresh strawberries, consider certain appearance points. Good-quality strawberries are bright red, plump, and have a fragrant aroma. Unlike other berry varieties, the stem caps of strawberries should be attached. Large berries, although appealing, are not necessarily the sweetest or best-flavored.

Other easily recognizable features point to berries that should be avoided. Those strawberries that are spotted with white areas may redden if left on a sunny sill, but they will never ripen in flavor. Reject, too, those berries that are misshapen, bruised, or moldy.

## How to store

Strawberries will maintain top quality longer if you handle them gently, and as little as possible. Although strawberries may be washed prior to storage if they are dried on toweling, many people prefer to wash them just prior to use.

If you intend to use the berries within a short time after purchase, lightly cover them and refrigerator-store them for a day or two. If the quantity of berries that you have on hand is more than you can use immediately, consider freezing them, sweetened or unsweetened, or preserving them in delicious jelly, jam, preserve, or conserve products.

To prevent the strawberries from crushing one another while they are in storage, transfer them to a flat, shallow container. Discard berries that are misshapen.

To wash the strawberries, add the berries with stem caps on to a pan of cold water. With your fingers, swirl the berries slowly, then lift them out and drain.

A tweezerlike strawberry huller is the ideal tool for removing strawberry stem caps. The job moves along quickly, this way and you have minimum waste.

# How to use

Since the colonists first raved about the great quantity and delicious flavor of the wild strawberries that they found growing in the United States, strawberry recipes have developed in profusion. In those days, fresh berries had to be used immediately, often on cereal or for dessert. Preparation of jellies, jams, and preserves was necessary if strawberries were to be enjoyed for the remainder of the year. Today, we still enjoy the pleasures of strawberries atop cereal or with cream, in addition to fancier recipes suitable in between and during mealtime.

## Strawberry Shake

*Low-cal version—*

**2 cups fresh *or* frozen, unsweetened, whole strawberries**
**1½ cups skim milk**
**2 tablespoons sugar**
**Dash ground cinnamon**

If using fresh strawberries, halve larger berries; freeze in plastic bag. In blender container combine milk, sugar, and ground cinnamon; gradually add frozen strawberries. Blend on medium speed till mixture is smooth. Serve shakes immediately. Makes 5 servings.

***Freezing strawberries***

Although strawberries may be frozen without added sweetening, the sweetened fruit is generally better quality. Wash berries; drain and remove hulls. Slice or leave whole. Then sugar pack or syrup pack.

*Sugar pack*—Add ¾ cup sugar for each quart of berries; mix well. Place in containers, leaving headspace. (One-half inch per pint for wide top opening; ¾ inch per pint for narrow opening.) Seal; label; freeze.

*Syrup pack*—Prepare syrup by dissolving 4¾ cups sugar in 4 cups boiling water; chill. Place berries in containers; cover with cold syrup. Leave headspace. Seal; label; freeze.

## Cherry-Strawberry Jam

**1 20-ounce can pitted tart red cherries (water pack)**
**1 10-ounce package frozen, sliced strawberries, thawed**
**4½ cups sugar**
**3 tablespoons lemon juice**
**½ 6-ounce bottle liquid fruit pectin**

Drain cherries, reserving juice. Chop cherries; measure and add enough juice to make 2 cups. Combine cherries, strawberries, sugar, and lemon juice in large saucepan. Bring to *full, rolling boil; boil hard 1 minute,* stirring constantly. Remove from heat; stir in pectin at once. Skim off foam. Stir and skim for 5 minutes to prevent fruit from floating. Ladle quickly into hot, scalded jars. Seal the jars at once. Makes six ½-pint jars.

There are innumerable delectable desserts based on strawberries to tempt diners' palates. Strawberry shortcake is as closely linked with American cuisine as grandmother's apple pie. Pancakes and waffles with fresh strawberries or a strawberry-based sauce may be a specialty breakfast item or an elegant dessert in your household. Strawberry cakes, pies, dumplings, cobblers, and many others offer eye appeal and flavor, too.

## No-Bake Strawberry Shortcake

*A fast variation of a classic—*

**1 2-ounce package dessert topping mix *or* 1 cup whipping cream, sweetened and whipped**
**8 slices soft white bread**
**1 quart fresh strawberries, hulled**
**⅓ cup sugar**

Prepare dessert topping mix according to package directions. Trim crusts from bread; fit 4 *slices* in 8x8x2-inch baking dish. Mash berries; stir in sugar. Spoon *half* the berry mixture over bread in baking dish; spread *half* the dessert topping over berries. Repeat layers. Chill about 1 hour. Cut in squares. Makes 9 servings.

## *Berry-laden platter*

← Luscious strawberry sauce and marshmallow whipped cream are drizzled over butter-glazed pancakes for Spring Pancakes.

## Sunshine Shortcake

**2 tablespoons butter or margarine**
**1 8¾-ounce can crushed pineapple, drained**
**¼ cup brown sugar**
**2 cups packaged biscuit mix**
**2 tablespoons granulated sugar**
**1 beaten egg**
**⅔ cup light cream**
**¼ cup butter or margarine, melted**
**1 cup whipping cream**
**1 pint fresh strawberries, hulled, sliced, and sweetened**

In 9x1½-inch round pan, melt the 2 tablespoons butter. Stir in pineapple and brown sugar; spread evenly in pan. In mixing bowl combine biscuit mix and next 4 ingredients; mix well with a fork, then beat vigorously 30 seconds. Spoon evenly over pineapple mixture, spreading dough to edges of pan. Bake at 450° for 15 minutes. Cool 1 minute; invert onto serving plate. Cut in wedges. Whip cream; top each serving with cream and strawberries. Makes 6 servings.

## Strawberry-Lemonade Bavarian

**1 envelope unflavored gelatin**
**¼ cup cold water**
**½ cup boiling water**
**1 6-ounce can frozen lemonade concentrate, thawed (⅔ cup)**
**1 10-ounce package frozen strawberries, partially thawed**
**1 cup whipping cream**

Soften gelatin in cold water; dissolve in boiling water. Stir in concentrate and berries with juice. Chill till partially set. Whip cream. Fold into gelatin. Pour into six ½-cup molds. Chill till firm. Unmold; top with whipped cream and mint leaves, if desired. Serves 6.

## Crepes Ambrosia

**½ cup sifted all-purpose flour**
**¾ cup milk**
**2 eggs**
**1½ tablespoons sugar**
**Dash salt**
**3 drops vanilla**
**2 cups hulled, fresh strawberries**
**2 tablespoons sugar**
**¼ cup kirsch**
**¼ cup orange-flavored liqueur**
**Vanilla ice cream**
**2 cups hulled, fresh strawberries**

Combine flour, milk, eggs, the 1½ tablespoons sugar, salt, and vanilla; beat with rotary beater till smooth. Refrigerate several hours to let the mixture thicken a little.

Heat heavy 6-inch skillet till a drop of water dances on the surface. Then, grease lightly and pour in 2 tablespoons batter. Lift skillet off heat and tilt from side to side till batter covers bottom evenly. Cook till underside of crepe is lightly browned. Cook on one side only. Repeat with remaining batter, using 2 tablespoons batter for each crepe. Keep warm.

Mash the first 2 cups strawberries in chafing dish over direct heat or in a 9-inch skillet over low heat. Add the 2 tablespoons sugar, kirsch, and liqueur; heat just to boiling. Stir and set aflame. Add crepes; simmer, uncovered, for about 3 minutes.

Place a scoop of ice cream in each of 10 dessert dishes; surround the ice cream with remaining strawberries. Place a crepe over each serving of ice cream and strawberries; top with some of strawberry syrup. Makes 10 servings.

## Spring Pancakes

**2 cups sifted all-purpose flour**
**5 teaspoons baking powder**
**2 teaspoons sugar**
**½ teaspoon salt**
**2 cups milk**
**½ cup light cream**
**2 beaten eggs**
**¼ cup butter or margarine, melted**
**Butter or margarine, melted**
**Brown sugar**
**Marshmallow Cream**
**Strawberry Sauce**

Sift together flour, baking powder, sugar, and salt. Combine milk, cream, eggs, and butter. Add to dry ingredients; beat smooth. Using ⅓ cup batter for each pancake, bake 6-inch pancakes on hot griddle. Keep warm in very slow oven on towel-covered pan.

To serve the pancakes, brush pancakes with melted butter; sprinkle with brown sugar (1 teaspoon each); stack them on a warm platter. Spoon Marshmallow Cream atop pancakes. Drizzle with Strawberry Sauce; trim pancakes with additional berries, if desired. Serves 6.

*Marshmallow Cream:* Mix one 1-pint jar marshmallow creme and ¼ cup softened butter or margarine. Whip ½ cup whipping cream; fold it into marshmallow mixture.

*Strawberry Sauce:* Reserving a few strawberries for trim, halve or quarter 1 quart hulled, fresh strawberries. Mix berries with ½ cup sugar; heat mixture to boiling.

## Strawberry Dumplings

*Home-style eating is at its best when this dish is served with cream—*

**⅓ cup sugar**
**⅔ cup water**
**½ teaspoon vanilla**

• • •

**1 cup sifted all-purpose flour**
**2 tablespoons sugar**
**1½ teaspoons baking powder**
**½ teaspoon salt**
**¼ cup butter or margarine**
**½ cup milk**

• • •

**1 pint fresh strawberries, hulled**
**1 tablespoon sugar**

In saucepan combine the ⅓ cup sugar and water. Bring mixture to boiling; reduce heat and simmer, uncovered, 5 minutes. Stir in vanilla. Sift together flour, the 2 tablespoons sugar, baking powder, and salt. Cut in butter or margarine till mixture is crumbly. Add milk and stir just till well combined.

Place berries in 1½-quart casserole; pour hot sugar mixture over. Immediately drop dumpling dough in 8 to 10 spoonfuls over berries. Sprinkle dumplings with remaining sugar. Bake at 450° till dumplings are done, 25 to 30 minutes. Serve warm. Makes 4 or 5 servings.

## Berry-Orange Coffee Cake

*Make this a breakfast finale—*

**1 cup sifted all-purpose flour**
**2 tablespoons sugar**
**1½ teaspoons baking powder**
**½ teaspoon salt**
**¼ cup butter or margarine**
**1 beaten egg**
**⅓ cup milk**
**½ 10-ounce package frozen strawberries, thawed (½ cup)**
**¼ cup orange marmalade**
**Topping**

Sift together flour, sugar, baking powder, and salt; cut in butter till crumbly. Combine egg and milk; add to dry ingredients and stir till moistened. Spread in an 8x8x2-inch baking pan. Blend berries with marmalade. Spoon over dough. Sprinkle with Topping.

*Topping:* Combine ¼ cup sugar and 3 tablespoons all-purpose flour; cut in ¼ cup butter or margarine till mixture is crumbly. Bake at 400° for 30 to 35 minutes.

## Strawberry Crunch Cake

**2 cups sifted all-purpose flour**
**4 teaspoons baking powder**
**⅓ cup sugar**
**¾ teaspoon salt**
**⅓ cup shortening**
**⅔ cup milk**
**1 slightly beaten egg**
**2 cups sliced, hulled, fresh strawberries**
**½ cup sugar**
**¼ cup butter or margarine, softened**
**¼ cup sugar**
**⅓ cup all-purpose flour**

Sift together flour, baking powder, the ⅓ cup sugar, and salt; cut in shortening. Combine milk and egg; stir into flour mixture. Blend well. Spread in greased 11x7x1½-inch pan.

Spoon strawberries over batter; sprinkle with the ½ cup sugar. Mix butter, the ¼ cup sugar, and ⅓ cup flour; crumble over berries. Bake at 425° for 35 to 40 minutes. Serve warm with ice cream, if desired. Makes 8 servings.

## Strawberry Glamour Pie

**2 egg whites**
**½ teaspoon vinegar**
**¼ teaspoon salt**
**⅓ cup sugar**
**1 *baked* 9-inch pastry shell (See *Pastry*)**
**2 cups sliced, hulled, fresh strawberries**
**¼ cup sugar**
**1 tablespoon cornstarch**
**½ cup cold water**
**Few drops red food coloring**
**½ cup whipping cream**

Beat egg whites with vinegar and salt to soft peaks. Gradually add ⅓ cup sugar, beating to stiff peaks. Spread on bottom and sides of pastry shell. Bake at 325° for 12 minutes; cool.

Mash ½ *cup* berries with ¼ cup sugar. Combine cornstarch and water; stir in mashed berries. Cook and stir till mixture boils; cook 2 minutes longer. Stir in food coloring and remaining berries; cool slightly. Spread over meringue; chill. Whip cream; spread over pie.

Ever think of poking holes in a freshly baked cake? That's what you do to give Pink Cloud Cake its moistness and flavor.

## Strawberry Tarts

**1 cup sugar**
**2 tablespoons cornstarch**
**1 quart fresh strawberries, hulled**
• • •
**1 tablespoon butter or margarine**
**1 3-ounce package strawberry-flavored gelatin**
**1 tablespoon lemon juice**
**6 to 8 *baked* Tart Shells, cooled (See *Pastry*)**

In saucepan combine sugar and cornstarch. Mash *1 cup* of the berries; add water to make 2 cups. Stir into sugar mixture. Cook and stir till boiling; boil 2 minutes. Remove from heat.

Add butter, gelatin, and lemon juice; stir till gelatin dissolves. Chill till partially set. Spoon ⅓ of the gelatin mixture into shells; top with the whole berries. Spoon remaining gelatin over berries; chill.

## Strawberry-Cheese Pie

**1 cup miniature marshmallows**
**½ cup milk**
**1 3-ounce package strawberry-flavored gelatin**
**½ cup water**
**1 3-ounce package cream cheese, softened**
• • •
**1 10-ounce package frozen strawberries, thawed**
**½ cup whipping cream**
**1 *baked* 9-inch pastry shell (See *Pastry*)**

In saucepan heat marshmallows and milk over medium-low heat, stirring frequently, till marshmallows are melted; cool. In small saucepan combine gelatin and water; heat and stir till gelatin is dissolved. Combine cooled marshmallow mixture and gelatin; gradually beat into softened cream cheese.

Drain berries, reserving syrup. Add enough water to syrup to make 1 cup liquid. Stir syrup into gelatin mixture; chill till partially set. Whip gelatin mixture; fold in berries. Whip cream; fold into whipped gelatin mixture. Pour into pastry shell. Chill firm. Trim with additional cream and berries, if desired.

## Strawberry Glaze Pie

**4 cups hulled, fresh strawberries**
**1 cup water**
**¾ cup sugar**
**3 tablespoons cornstarch**
**Few drops red food coloring**
**1 *baked* and cooled 8-inch pastry shell (See *Pastry*)**
**Whipped cream**

Crush *1 cup* strawberries and cook with water about 2 minutes; sieve. Combine sugar and cornstarch; stir into berry juice. Cook and stir till thickened and bubbly. Add food coloring.

Place *1½ cups* strawberries in pastry shell. Pour *half* the sauce over. Repeat layers with remaining berries and sauce. Chill. Garnish the pie with whipped cream.

## Strawberry Scrumptious

*Four unique layers—*

**1½ cups finely crushed vanilla wafers**
**5 tablespoons sugar**
**¼ cup butter or margarine, melted**
**4 egg whites**
**½ cup sugar**
**1 pint fresh strawberries, hulled and sliced**
**1 cup whipping cream**

Combine crumbs, *2 tablespoons* sugar, and butter. Press into 8x8x2-inch baking dish. In large mixing bowl beat whites till soft peaks form. Gradually add ½ cup sugar, beating to stiff peaks. Spread meringue over crumbs. Bake at 350° for 15 to 17 minutes; cool.

Sprinkle strawberries with remaining 3 tablespoons sugar. Let stand 10 to 15 minutes; drain. Whip cream; spread over meringue. Top with strawberries; chill. Makes 8 or 9 servings.

## *Spectacular finale*

Ladle flaming liquor over Berries and Nectarines au Rum to transform this simple fruit sauce into an elegant dessert. →

Adorn each individual mold of Strawberry-Lemonade Bavarian with a generous mound of whipped cream and a sprig of fresh mint.

## Strawberry Frozen Pie

**1 8-ounce package cream cheese, softened**
**1 cup dairy sour cream**
• • •
**2 10-ounce packages frozen, sliced strawberries, thawed**
**1 9-inch Graham Cracker Crust (See *Crumb Crust*)**

Blend cream cheese and sour cream. Reserve ½ cup berries (and syrup); add remaining berries and syrup to cheese mixture. Pour into crust. Freeze till firm. Remove from freezer 5 minutes before serving. Cut in wedges; serve topped with reserved berries in syrup.

## Lush Strawberry Meringue Pie

**3 egg whites**
**¼ teaspoon cream of tartar**
**1 cup sugar**
• • •
**4 cups halved, hulled, fresh strawberries**
**2 cups whipping cream**
**¼ cup sugar**

Beat egg whites and cream of tartar *just* till soft peaks form. Gradually add 1 cup sugar, beating to stiff peaks. Spread in a 9-inch pie plate, mounding sides high. Bake at 275° for 60 minutes. Turn oven off; leave meringue in oven till it cools. Fill shell with *half* the strawberries. Whip cream with ¼ cup sugar. Spread over strawberries in shell; garnish with remaining berries. Chill pie well, 3 to 4 hours; serve pie in wedges.

## Strawberry Ribbon Pie

**2 tablespoons sugar**
**2 tablespoons cornstarch**
**1 envelope unflavored gelatin (1 tablespoon)**
**¼ cup water**
**¼ cup lemon juice**
**1 16-ounce package frozen strawberries, thawed**
**1 9-inch Graham Cracker Crust (See *Crumb Crust*)**
**2 egg whites**
**¼ teaspoon cream of tartar**
**¼ cup sugar**
**1 cup whipping cream**

In saucepan combine the 2 tablespoons sugar, cornstarch, and gelatin. Stir in water and lemon juice; add strawberries. Cook, stirring constantly, till mixture is thickened and bubbly. Chill till partially set.

Pour *half* the mixture into pie shell. Beat egg whites and cream of tartar to soft peaks. Gradually add the ¼ cup sugar, beating to stiff peaks. Whip *half* the whipping cream. Fold remaining strawberry mixture and whipped cream into beaten egg whites. Spread atop gelatin in shell. Chill till firm. To serve, whip remaining cream and use as garnish.

Many fruit lovers agree that fresh strawberries used in fruit cups and salads produce more elegant food flair than so-called gourmet recipes. Strawberries swimming in bubbly champagne have a simple, yet epicurean appeal. Assorted fruits including strawberries serve as convenient and tasty dippers at appetizer time. Fruit plates and molded salads using strawberries are also menu features.

## Berries and Nectarines au Rum

**2 cups hulled, fresh strawberries**
**1/4 cup sugar**
**1 teaspoon cornstarch**
**1 cup sliced, peeled nectarines**
**1/4 cup rum**
**Vanilla ice cream**

Mash *1 cup* strawberries. Halve remaining berries. In blazer pan of chafing dish, stir together sugar and cornstarch; gradually stir in purėed berries. Cook and stir over medium heat till mixture is thickened; add the halved berries and sliced nectarines. Return to boiling. Heat rum in ladle or small pan; flame and pour over fruit sauce. Serve over vanilla ice cream. Makes about 2 cups sauce.

## Fruit Melange

**1 16-ounce can pitted dark sweet cherries, drained and halved**
**1 pint fresh strawberries, hulled and sliced**
**1 medium cantaloupe, cut in balls**
**1 12½-ounce can pineapple chunks, drained**
**1/2 cup orange marmalade**
**1/4 cup hot water**
**1 teaspoon finely chopped, candied ginger**
**1 medium-large banana, sliced**
**Fresh mint leaves**

Chill fruits; layer cherries, strawberries, melon, and pineapple in compote or large glass bowl. Combine orange marmalade, hot water, and candied ginger. Drizzle over fruit. Chill.

Arrange banana atop fruit mixture. (To keep banana from darkening, dip in ascorbic acid color keeper or lemon juice mixed with a little water.) Garnish with mint. Serves 12.

## Quick Fruit Dip

Combine one 8-ounce carton yogurt, 3 tablespoons low-calorie strawberry jam, and 1/4 teaspoon ground cinnamon; chill. Serve with chilled fruit dippers: seedless green grapes, apple wedges, cantaloupe or honeydew balls, or pineapple chunks. Makes about 1 1/4 cups.

## Strawberries Juliet

Using 2½ cups fresh strawberries, chilled, crush *1/4 cup* of the berries; halve remaining berries. Combine crushed berries; 1/3 cup frozen, whipped dessert topping, thawed; 1/3 cup yogurt; and 1 tablespoon sugar. Spoon halved berries into 4 sherbet glasses; top with strawberry-yogurt mixture. Makes 4 servings.

## Fresh Fruit Aloha

*Strawberries team with pineapple and papaya—*

**1 cup fresh pineapple chunks**
**1 papaya, peeled, seeded, and cubed**
**1/2 cup sliced strawberries**
**1 teaspoon lime juice**
**2 tablespoons sugar**

Combine pineapple, papaya, and strawberries; sprinkle with the lime juice and *1 tablespoon* of the sugar. Chill mixture thoroughly. Just before serving, sprinkle fruits with the second tablespoon sugar. Serve as an appetizer or as a dessert. Makes 4 servings.

## Strawberry Yogurt Salad

*Another time pour into individual molds—*

**1 8¾-ounce can crushed pineapple**
**1 envelope unflavored gelatin (1 tablespoon)**
**1 8-ounce carton strawberry-flavored yogurt (1 cup)**
**Dash salt**
**1 10-ounce package frozen strawberries, thawed**
**Lettuce**

Drain pineapple, reserving syrup. In saucepan soften gelatin in the pineapple syrup. Stir over low heat till gelatin is dissolved. Stir into strawberry-flavored yogurt with dash salt. Add thawed strawberries, including syrup and drained pineapple. Mix well. Pour into a 4½-cup mold; chill till firm. Unmold onto lettuce-lined plate. Garnish with more strawberries, if desired. Makes 4 to 6 servings.

## Strawberry Cups

*Double strawberry flavor—*

**1 8¾-ounce can pineapple tidbits**
**1 cup fresh, halved, hulled strawberries***
**2 tablespoons sugar**

• • •

**1 3-ounce package strawberry-flavored gelatin**
**2 tablespoons lemon juice**
**Dash salt**

Drain pineapple, reserving ½ cup syrup. Combine strawberries and sugar; chill till juice forms. Drain, reserving juice; heat to boiling with enough water to make 1¼ cups. Dissolve gelatin in boiling juice. Stir in reserved pineapple syrup, lemon juice, and salt. Chill till partially set. Fold in pineapple tidbits and strawberry halves. Pour into six ½-cup molds; chill till firm. Makes 6 servings.

*Or use two 10-ounce packages frozen, sliced strawberries, thawed; drain, reserving 1 cup juice. Bring juice to boiling. Dissolve the gelatin in the boiling juice.

## Banana-Strawberry Freeze

**1 10-ounce package frozen strawberries, partially thawed**
**¼ cup lemon juice**

• • •

**1 fully ripe banana, quartered**
**⅔ cup sugar**
**1 cup whipping cream**

Break up frozen strawberries into blender container. Add lemon juice. Blend till smooth. Add banana and sugar; blend. Pour into mixing bowl. Whip cream; fold into fruit.

Freeze in refrigerator trays overnight, or till firm. Makes 5 or 6 servings.

The flavor of strawberries has been incorporated into many convenience foods. Strawberry-flavored gelatin, strawberry ice cream, whipped strawberry desserts, and even strawberry cake mix are only a few of the many examples. (See *Berry, Fruit* for additional information.)

## Strawberry Meringue Puffs

**2 egg whites**
**½ teaspoon vanilla**
**½ cup sugar**
**4 sponge cake dessert cups**
**1 pint strawberry ice cream**
**1 10-ounce package frozen strawberries, thawed**

Beat egg whites and vanilla till soft peaks form. Gradually add sugar, beating to stiff peaks. Spread meringue on top and sides of each sponge cake cup. Place on baking sheet; bake at 450° for 5 minutes. Remove from oven; fill center of each cup with a scoop of ice cream. Spoon berries over. Makes 4 servings.

## Pink Cloud Cake

**1 package 2-layer-size white cake mix**
**1 3-ounce package strawberry-flavored gelatin**
**1 cup boiling water**
**½ cup cold water**

• • •

**1 16-ounce package frozen strawberry halves, thawed**
**1 3½-ounce package strawberry whipped dessert mix**
**1 2- or 2⅛-ounce package dessert topping mix**

Prepare cake according to package directions. Bake in two 9x1½-inch round pans.* Dissolve gelatin in boiling water; stir in cold water. Set aside for 20 minutes. Cool cake in pans 5 minutes. Remove; place on racks over waxed paper. Using long-tined fork, punch holes in cake, making even rows across cake surface. Spoon gelatin over cake; chill 1 to 2 hours.

Drain berries, reserving ½ cup syrup. Using berry syrup for the ½ cup water, prepare whipped dessert mix according to package directions. Fold in berries. Spread *1 cup* whipped dessert mix atop one cake layer. Place second layer atop filling. Frost entire cake with remaining whipped dessert mix. Chill 1 hour. Prepare dessert topping mix according to package directions; spread over the pink layer.

*Or bake in 13x9x2-inch baking pan according to package directions. Leave in pan.

## Strawberry Cake Roll

**3/4 cup sifted cake flour**
**3/4 teaspoon baking powder**
**1/4 teaspoon salt**
**4 eggs**
**1 teaspoon vanilla**
**3/4 cup sugar**
**Confectioners' sugar**

• • •

**1 3-ounce package strawberry-flavored gelatin**
**1 cup boiling water**
**1 10-ounce package frozen strawberries**
**1 2- or 2 1/8-ounce package dessert topping mix**

Sift together flour, baking powder, and salt. Beat eggs and vanilla till thick and lemon-colored. Gradually add sugar, beating till fluffy. Fold in flour mixture. Spread batter evenly in greased and lightly floured 15½x10½x1-inch jelly roll pan. Bake at 400° till lightly browned, 10 to 12 minutes. Immediately loosen sides; turn onto towel sprinkled with confectioners' sugar. Starting at narrow end, roll cake and towel together; cool 30 minutes on rack. Chill the cake thoroughly.

For filling, dissolve gelatin in boiling water; stir in frozen berries till thawed. Chill till partially set. Unroll cake. Spread with gelatin mixture; place in refrigerator till gelatin mixture is *almost* firm, about 10 minutes. Carefully reroll cake. Chill several hours. Prepare dessert topping mix according to package directions; frost cake roll. Store in refrigerator until serving time.

## Triple Strawberry Compote

*A quick, yet unique dessert—*

**1 quart fresh strawberries, hulled and halved**
**1 pint strawberry ice cream**
**1 8-ounce carton strawberry yogurt (1 cup)**

Spoon strawberries into large compote or individual sherbets. Stir ice cream just to soften; fold in yogurt. Drizzle ice cream mixture over berries. Makes 8 servings.

Strawberry Dumplings—another colorful recipe idea that presents the fresh berries in a different, yet quick, flavorful way.

## Rosy Strawberry Ring

**2 3-ounce packages strawberry-flavored gelatin**
**2 cups boiling water**
**2 10-ounce packages frozen, sliced strawberries**

• • •

**1 13½-ounce can crushed pineapple**
**2 large, ripe bananas, peeled and finely diced**
**2 tablespoons lemon juice**

• • •

**1 cup dairy sour cream**
**1 teaspoon sugar**
**1/4 teaspoon ground ginger**
**Dash salt**

Dissolve gelatin in boiling water. Add berries, stirring occasionally until thawed. Stir in pineapple, banana, and lemon juice. Pour into a 6½-cup mold. Chill till firm.

Meanwhile, in small bowl combine sour cream, sugar, ginger, and salt. Chill well. Pass dressing with salad. Makes 8 servings.

## Strawberry Delight

**1 11¼-ounce frozen loaf pound cake, thawed**
**3 3-ounce packages strawberry-flavored gelatin**
**2 16-ounce packages frozen sliced strawberries**
**2 cups whipping cream**

Cut pound cake crosswise into 16 thin slices. Fit cake slices into the bottoms of two 9x9x2-inch baking pans. In large bowl dissolve strawberry gelatin in 3 cups boiling water. Add frozen strawberries and let stand till berries are thawed and gelatin thickens slightly. Stir occasionally. Whip cream just till soft peaks form. Fold into partially set gelatin mixture. If necessary, chill till mixture mounds. Pour *half* the strawberry mixture over pound cake in *each* pan. Chill several hours or overnight. To serve, cut into squares. Serves 18.

## Strawberry Swirl

**1 cup graham cracker crumbs**
**1 tablespoon sugar**
**¼ cup butter or margarine, melted**
**. . .**
**1 3-ounce package strawberry-flavored gelatin**
**1 cup boiling water**
**1 cup cold water**
**8 ounces marshmallows**
**½ cup milk**
**1 cup whipping cream**
**2 cups sliced fresh strawberries**

Mix crumbs, sugar, and melted butter. Press mixture firmly over the bottom of a 9x9x2-inch baking pan. Chill till crumbs are set.

Dissolve strawberry-flavored gelatin in the 1 cup boiling water. Add the cold water. Chill till gelatin mixture is partially set.

Meanwhile, in saucepan combine marshmallows and milk; heat and stir till marshmallows melt. Cool thoroughly. Whip cream just till peaks begin to form; fold into cooled marshmallow mixture. Add berries to gelatin, then swirl in marshmallow mixture to marble. Pour into crust and chill till set in refrigerator. Cut into squares to serve. Garnish with additional whipped cream, if desired. Serves 9 to 12.

## Pink Parfaits

**1 3-ounce package strawberry-flavored gelatin**
**1 10-ounce package frozen sliced strawberries**
**1 cup strawberry ice cream**

In blender container combine gelatin and ¾ cup boiling water. Cover and blend at high speed till gelatin is dissolved, about 20 seconds. Cut package of frozen strawberries in half; allow *half* to thaw for topping. Add remaining strawberries to gelatin; blend till nearly smooth. Add ice cream, a spoonful at a time, blending till smooth after each addition. Pour mixture into 4 parfait glasses; chill in freezer at least 10 minutes. To serve, garnish with thawed strawberries. Makes 4 servings.

## Strawberry Soufflé Salads

Thaw and drain one 10-ounce package frozen sliced strawberries; reserve syrup. Add water to syrup to make ¾ cup. Dissolve one 3-ounce package strawberry-flavored gelatin and ¼ teaspoon salt in 1 cup boiling water. Add reserved syrup and 2 tablespoons lemon juice. Beat in ¼ cup mayonnaise. Chill till partially set. Whip with electric mixer till fluffy. Fold in berries and ¼ cup chopped walnuts. Pour into individual molds. Chill till set. Unmold on lettuce. Makes 4 to 6 servings.

## Strawberry-Banana Ice

**1 4-serving envelope low-calorie strawberry-flavored gelatin**
**2 tablespoons lemon juice**
**¾ teaspoon rum flavoring**
**1 10-ounce package frozen strawberries, thawed**
**1 fully ripe medium banana, mashed**

Dissolve gelatin in 1 cup boiling water; stir in ¾ cup cold water, lemon juice, and rum flavoring. Stir berries and banana into gelatin. Pour mixture into two 4-cup freezer trays. Freeze firm. Break into chunks. In chilled bowl beat *half* the mixture with electric mixer till smooth. Return to tray. Repeat with remaining mixture. Freeze firm. Serves 10.

**STREUSEL** ***(stroi' zuhl, stro͞o-')***—A crumbly topping made of flour, sugar, and butter, often with spices, such as cinnamon, and nuts added. The mixture is sprinkled on coffee cakes, muffins, and pies. Its name is derived from the German word that means to strew or to sprinkle.

## Streusel Coffee Cake

**1 package active dry yeast**
**3½ cups sifted all-purpose flour**
**1¼ cups milk**
**¼ cup granulated sugar**
**¼ cup shortening**
**1 teaspoon salt**
**1 egg**

• • •

**1 cup sifted all-purpose flour**
**½ cup brown sugar**
**½ cup granulated sugar**
**1 teaspoon ground cinnamon**
**½ cup butter or margarine**
**¼ cup finely chopped nuts**
**1½ teaspoons vanilla**

*To prepare coffee cake,* combine yeast and *2 cups* of the flour in large mixer bowl. Heat milk, ¼ cup sugar, shortening, and salt just till warm, stirring occasionally to melt shortening. Add to dry mixture in bowl; add egg. Beat at low speed with electric mixer for ½ minute, scraping sides of bowl constantly. Beat 3 minutes at high speed. By hand stir in remaining 1½ cups flour to make a soft dough. Place in greased bowl, turning to grease surface. Cover and let rise till double, 1½ to 2 hours. Turn out on floured surface; divide in thirds. Pat each into greased 8x1½-inch round pan. Sprinkle a third of the topping over each cake. Cover; let rise till double, 30 to 45 minutes. Bake at 375° till done, 20 minutes. Immediately drizzle ½ *teaspoon* vanilla over each coffee cake. Serve warm. Makes 3 cakes.

*To prepare streusel topping,* mix 1 cup all-purpose flour, brown sugar, ½ cup granulated sugar, and cinnamon; cut in butter till the streusel topping is crumbly. Add nuts.

**STRING BEAN**—The former name for green beans. Before the development of crossbreeds, beans had a string or thread running along the side, which had to be removed before cooking. Today, most beans sold are stringless. (See also *Bean.*)

**STRIPED BASS**—A type of bass that has black stripes on each side of the body. This species of fish is found on both coasts of America. On the East Coast, striped bass is also called rockfish. Formerly, the striped bass was native only to the East Coast, but in 1879 it was transported across the continent by train. Now, both the eastern and western fish are considered good game fish. Striped bass measure 15 to 18 inches in length and can weigh up to as much as 40 pounds. The common market size is about four pounds.

Whole striped bass and fillets are available all year in both fresh and frozen forms. Since it is a lean fish, striped bass is often poached, steamed, or fried. However, it can be broiled or baked if it is kept moist with shortening or sauce during cooking. (See also *Fish.*)

## Mint-Stuffed Striped Bass

**1 4-pound fresh or frozen, dressed striped bass**
**3 cups dry bread cubes (4 slices)**
**1 tablespoon snipped, fresh mint or 1 teaspoon dried mint leaves, crushed**
**½ teaspoon salt**
**¼ teaspoon dried basil leaves, crushed**
**1 clove garlic, minced**
**3 tablespoons butter or margarine**
**2 teaspoons lemon juice**
**2 tablespoons salad oil**
**2 tablespoons lemon juice**

Thaw frozen fish. Place in well-greased, shallow baking pan. Combine bread cubes, mint, ½ teaspoon salt, basil, and dash pepper. In small saucepan cook garlic in butter 1 minute. Add to stuffing mixture with ¼ cup water and 2 teaspoons lemon juice; toss lightly. Stuff fish loosely with mixture. Combine salad oil and 2 tablespoons lemon juice. Brush fish with mixture. Bake at 350° till fish flakes easily when tested with a fork, 50 to 60 minutes. Baste occasionally with oil mixture. Serves 8.

## Cheese-Sauced Striped Bass

*Elegant enough for a company dinner—*

Use 2 pounds fresh or frozen striped bass fillets; thaw frozen fish. Cut into 6 portions. Place in shallow baking dish.

In saucepan melt 1/4 cup butter or margarine. Blend in 1/4 cup all-purpose flour, 1/4 teaspoon garlic salt, and dash pepper. Add 1 1/2 cups milk and 1/2 cup dry white wine. Cook and stir till thickened and bubbly. Stir in 1 tablespoon grated Parmesan cheese. Pour sauce over fish. Bake at 350° till fish flakes easily when tested with a fork, 20 to 25 minutes.

Sprinkle 2 tablespoons grated Parmesan cheese and dash paprika over top. Place under broiler just till cheese is browned and sauce is slightly bubbly, 1 minute. Makes 6 servings.

## Deviled Bass Fillets

Use 2 pounds fresh or frozen striped bass fillets; thaw frozen fish. Cut into 6 portions. Place on greased rack of broiler pan. Combine 1/4 cup chili sauce, 3 tablespoons melted butter, 2 tablespoons snipped chives, 1 tablespoon prepared mustard, 1/2 teaspoon salt, and dash bottled hot pepper sauce. Brush sauce over fish. Broil 4 inches from heat till fish flakes easily when tested with a fork, 10 to 15 minutes. Brush occasionally with sauce. Serves 6.

**STROGANOFF** ***(strô' guh nôf', strō-')***—The name of a delectable main dish including meat and a sauce composed of sour cream, a variety of seasonings, and often mushrooms. Stroganoff is frequently

Jiffy Stroganoff is a variation of the classic Russian recipe. Ground beef is substituted for the strips of steak, and sour cream sauce mix combined with milk adds creamy tanginess.

Prepare Beef Stroganoff at the table in a chafing dish. Brown meat and cook onion mixture in the blazer pan over direct flame. Remove meat mixture to a warm platter. Then, prepare sauce in the blazer pan. Return meat and mushroom mixture to the blazer pan. Stir in sour cream and wine. Keep warm over the hot water bath (bain-marie).

served over noodles. This famous dish is named for a gourmet, Count P. Stroganoff, a nineteenth-century Russian diplomat.

There are many variations of the classic dish. Some Americanized versions are modified, and occasionally you'll find economy variations made with ground beef instead of thin strips of tender beefsteak. (See also *Russian Cookery*.)

## Hamburger Stroganoff

**1 pound ground beef**
**3 slices bacon, diced**
**½ cup chopped onion**
**½ teaspoon salt**
**¼ teaspoon paprika**
**Dash pepper**
**1 10½-ounce can condensed cream of mushroom soup**
**1 cup dairy sour cream**
**Hot buttered noodles**

In skillet brown ground beef with bacon. Add onion; cook until tender but not brown. Drain off excess fat. Add salt, paprika, and dash pepper; stir in soup. Cook slowly, uncovered, 20 minutes, stirring frequently. Stir in sour cream. Heat, but *do not boil*. Serve over noodles. Makes 4 to 6 servings.

## Jiffy Stroganoff

**1 pound ground beef**
**2 tablespoons butter**
**2 tablespoons all-purpose flour**
**1 tablespoon instant minced onion**
**1 beef bouillon cube**
**½ teaspoon garlic salt**
**½ teaspoon paprika**

• • •

**1 3-ounce can sliced mushrooms**
**1 envelope sour cream sauce mix**
**1 6-ounce can evaporated milk**
**2 tablespoons dry sherry**
**Hot, buttered noodles**

Brown meat in butter. Stir in next 5 ingredients. Add 1 cup water and mushrooms with liquid. Cover; simmer 10 minutes. Combine sauce mix with milk; stir into meat. Add wine; heat. Serve over noodles. Makes 4 to 6 servings.

## Beef Stroganoff

**4 tablespoons all-purpose flour**
**1 pound beef sirloin, cut in ¼-inch strips**
**2 tablespoons butter or margarine**
**1 3-ounce can sliced mushrooms, drained**
**½ cup chopped onion**
**1 clove garlic, minced**
**2 tablespoons butter or margarine**
**1 tablespoon tomato paste**
**1¼ cups beef broth**
**1 cup dairy sour cream**
**2 tablespoons dry sherry**
**6 ounces noodles, cooked**

Combine *1 tablespoon* flour and ½ teaspoon salt; coat meat with mixture. Heat blazer pan of chafing dish or skillet; add 2 tablespoons butter. When melted, add meat; brown quickly on both sides. Add mushrooms, onion, and garlic; cook till onion is crisp-tender, 3 or 4 minutes. Remove meat and mushrooms.

Add 2 tablespoons butter or margarine to pan drippings; blend in 3 tablespoons all-purpose flour. Add tomato paste. Stir in cold beef broth. Cook and stir over medium-high heat till thickened and bubbly.

Return browned meat and mushrooms to blazer pan or skillet. Stir in sour cream and wine; cook slowly till heated through (do not boil). Keep warm over hot water. Serve over hot, buttered noodles. Makes 4 or 5 servings.

## Beer-Beef Stroganoff

In blazer pan of chafing dish quickly brown 2 pounds beef sirloin, cut in ¼-inch strips, in 2 tablespoons salad oil. Season with 1½ teaspoons salt and ⅛ teaspoon pepper. Remove meat from pan. In same pan cook, covered, 2 medium onions, sliced, and one 3-ounce can undrained mushrooms till onion is crisp-tender, 3 to 4 minutes. Push to one side.

Blend 2 tablespoons all-purpose flour and ¼ teaspoon paprika into pan drippings. Add 1½ cups beer and 1 teaspoon Worcestershire sauce; cook and stir till thickened and bubbly. Return meat to pan. Stir in 1 cup dairy sour cream; cook slowly till heated through (do not boil). Keep warm over hot water (bain-marie). Serve over hot, buttered noodles. Serves 6 to 8.

**STRUDEL** ***(strōōd' uhl)***—A pastry of German or Austrian origin. The word is derived from the German word meaning whirlpool, which is what the baked strudel looks like. This delicious pastry is made of paper-thin dough rolled over and over a filling of fruit, cheese, nuts, or poppy seeds so as to bake in many layers.

The dough, though the result is crisp and delicate, is quite elastic, and it is traditionally pulled on top of a table on a floured cloth to its paper-thin consistency. It's almost a necessity to enlist a helper for this part of strudelmaking. The thin dough, when sufficiently pulled, easily covers a large table.

After the desired filling has been spread near one edge of the dough and the small piece of dough has been folded over, the cloth is lifted along the same side so that the strudel rolls itself up into a tight roll. At this point, the strudel is baked till delicately browned.

An easier version, which omits the tedious process of stretching the dough to paper thinness, also can be prepared.

**A few chopped nuts sprinkled over the top and poached apple wedges garnish Quick Apple Strudel, a jiffy version of a classic.**

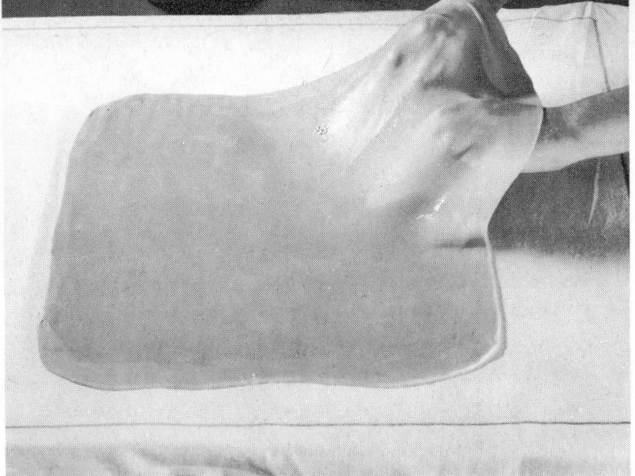

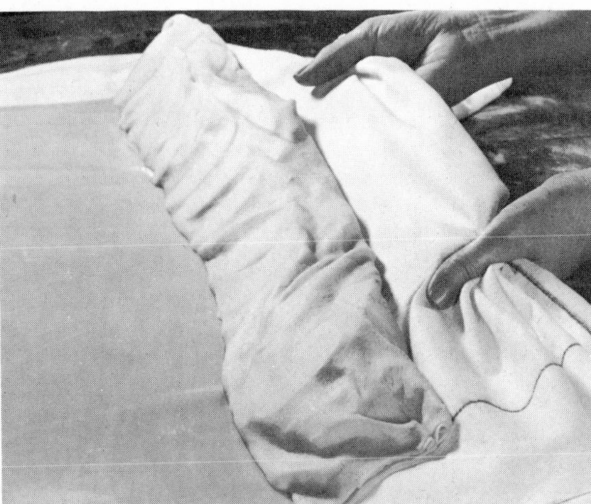

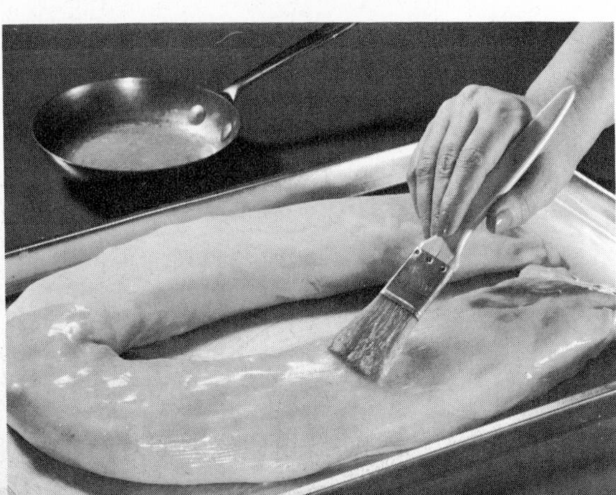

## *How to make apple strudel*

Stretch dough to paper thinness on a large table covered with a floured cloth. Use backs of hands, working underneath dough.

Arrange apples about six inches from the edge of one side of the dough. Sprinkle with cinnamon-sugar and half the currants.

After folding the six-inch piece of dough over apple filling, pick up cloth behind filling and slowly raise cloth to roll dough.

Seal ends and place in baking pan, curving to form a horseshoe shape. Brush top with melted butter, using a pastry brush.

## Apple Strudel

**3 cups sifted all-purpose flour**
**½ teaspoon salt**
**½ cup butter or margarine**
**¾ cup warm water**
**1 slightly beaten egg**
**1 cup butter or margarine, melted**
**4 or 5 apples, peeled, cored, and thinly sliced (6 cups)**
**1 cup sugar**
**2 teaspoons ground cinnamon**
**½ cup dried currants**
**Sifted confectioners' sugar**

To make the pastry, combine flour and salt. Cut in ½ cup butter as for pastry. Combine water and egg; add to flour and stir well. Turn the dough out on a lightly floured surface; knead 5 minutes. Divide in half; cover and let stand 30 minutes.

Cover large table with floured cloth. On cloth roll *half* of dough to a 15-inch square. Brush with *2 tablespoons* of the melted butter; let stand a few minutes. To stretch dough, use *back* of hands, working underneath dough. Start from middle of square; gently stretch from one corner to the next until dough is paper-thin—a 36-inch square. (Don't lift too high—it tears easily). Trim off thick edges.

(*Continued on next page.*)

Brush $\frac{1}{4}$ *cup* of the melted butter over dough. Place *half* the apples evenly along one side, about 6 inches from edge. Combine sugar and cinnamon; pour *half* over apples. Top with *half* of the currants. Fold the 6-inch piece of dough over filling. Pick up cloth behind filling; slowly and evenly raise cloth, making dough roll forward into a tight roll. Seal ends. Place on buttered 15½x10½x1-inch baking pan; curve, forming crescent or horseshoe shape.

Brush top with *2 tablespoons* of the melted butter. Repeat stretching and filling with other half of dough and fill with remaining ingredients. Bake strudels at 350° for 45 to 50 minutes. Remove from pan; cool on rack. Sprinkle with sifted confectioners' sugar.

## Quick Apple Strudel

*Saves time with a no-knead pastry—*

**1½ cups sifted all-purpose flour**
**¼ cup sugar**
**¼ teaspoon salt**
**½ cup butter or margarine**
**1 egg yolk**
**2 tablespoons milk**
**1 teaspoon lemon juice**

• • •

**¼ cup fine dry bread crumbs**
**¼ cup finely chopped walnuts**
**1 tablespoon butter or margarine melted**
**2 medium apples, peeled, cored, and thinly sliced (2 cups)**
**2 tablespoons butter or margarine, melted**
**2 teaspoons lemon juice**
**⅓ cup sugar**
**1 teaspoon ground cinnamon**
**¼ cup raisins**
**½ teaspoon grated lemon peel**

• • •

**1 slightly beaten egg white**

*For pastry*, sift together the 1½ cups flour, ¼ cup sugar, and salt. Cut in ½ cup butter as for pastry. Combine egg yolk, milk, and 1 teaspoon lemon juice; stir into flour mixture to form dough. On floured baking sheet, roll the dough to a 13x8-inch rectangle.

*To prepare filling*, combine bread crumbs, nuts, and *1 tablespoon* of the melted butter. Sprinkle over surface of rolled dough. Drizzle apples with remaining butter and 2 teaspoons lemon juice. Add ⅓ cup sugar, cinnamon, raisins, and lemon peel; toss gently till mixed. Place apple mixture down center of dough. Using a spatula to loosen dough from baking sheet, carefully fold one side of dough over filling, just a little past center. Then, fold over the other side, slightly overlapping the first. Brush edges with a little of the beaten egg white; seal. Brush top with remaining egg white. Bake at 400° till golden brown, 30 minutes. Loosen from baking sheet with spatula. Cool. Remove from baking sheet with two pancake turners, as strudel is very fragile.

For Quick Apple Strudel, roll out dough, then sprinkle with crumb mixture and arrange apple slices down center lengthwise.

Because the baked strudel is so fragile, lift it from baking sheet with two pancake turners to avoid breaking the strudel.